No Fear

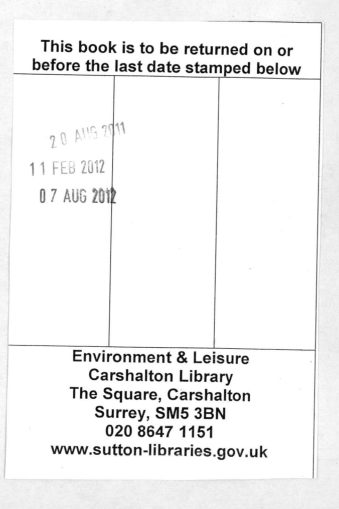

No Fear

Overcoming Anxiety and Panic Attacks

Alice Neville

HELP YOURSELF

Copyright © 2003 by Alice Neville

First published in Great Britain in 2003

The right of Alice Neville to be identified as the Author
of the Work has been asserted by her in accordance
with the Copyright, Designs and Patents Act 1988.

10 9 8 7 6 5 4 3 2

British Library Cataloguing in Publication Data
A record for this book is available from the British Library

ISBN 0 340 86133 9

Typeset in ACaslonRegular by Avon DataSet Ltd,
Bidford-on-Avon, Warwickshire

Printed and bound in Great Britain by
Bookmarque Ltd, Croydon, Surrey

The paper and board used in this paperback are natural recyclable products
made from wood grown in sustainable forests. The manufacturing processes
conform to the environmental regulations of the country of origin.

Hodder & Stoughton
A Division of Hodder Headline Ltd
338 Euston Road
London NW1 3BH
www.madaboutbooks.com

To past and present members of *The Open Door* and PAX, whose experiences and input to the newsletters have taught me much of what I know about the disorders I have covered in this book.

Contents

Preface

This book is based on my two earlier books, *Who's Afraid of Agoraphobia?* published by Arrow in 1986 and *Who's Afraid . . . ?* published by Arrow in 1991. These books are no longer in print but relevant passages are included here for new readers.

I would point out that the correct term for an agoraphobia sufferer is an 'agoraphobe', but as everyone else refers to them as 'agoraphobics' I have decided to conform.

The feminine pronoun is used most of the time simply because a great many of my contracts are women. I am not ignoring the fact that men are sufferers too, and I use 'he' or 'him' where appropriate.

Acknowledgements

With grateful thanks to the publishers McGraw Hill for permission to quote passages from Professor Isaac M. Marks' book *Living with Fear*.

I would also like to thank Peter Blythe and Sally Goddard Blythe for permission to quote from their paper *A Physical Basis for Agoraphobia*.

Introduction

I suffered from panic disorder and many phobias, including agoraphobia, from childhood until my mid-twenties. In 1965, long after I had recovered, I started a self-help organisation, *The Open Door*, to help agoraphobia sufferers through newsletters in which members pooled their knowledge of the problems and told other sufferers how they were coping, and what therapies were available. In the 1960s, treatments weren't very successful on the whole. This was the era of the tranquillisers which often did more harm than good and when many people became seriously addicted.

In recent years the condition known as panic disorder appears to have escalated. In 1990 a report by the Royal College of Psychiatrists stated that more than nine million people in the UK would suffer from abnormal anxiety and fears at some time in their lives.

In the 1980s I started another organisation – PAX – for panic disorders and phobias, and in recent years we have been joined by many other groups all over the country offering advice, telephone helplines, therapy groups, etc. Many produce their own newsletter and offer contact for other people with the same problem. Some are listed at the end of this book.

1

Panic attack

I pant, I sink, I tremble, I expire!
Shelley

The ambulance arrives at the A & E Department and a young woman is helped through the hospital doors. She is pale and shaking, and breathing erratically . . . a suspected heart attack. Hospital staff gently encourage her to calm down as they spend the next couple of hours putting her through a number of tests. Jane is terrified; such feelings as she has just experienced have never affected her before and she is convinced there is something terribly wrong – pains in her chest, ringing in her ears, faintness and dizziness and difficulty in getting her breath. These could be symptoms of a number of serious disorders.

'You can go home now, Jane,' the doctor tells her eventually. 'You have just experienced a severe anxiety attack. Nothing else wrong, just visit your GP in the next couple of days and he will prescribe something to settle your nerves.'

Jane sits and waits for her husband to collect her and take

her home. Her mind is spinning, and although she is partially comforted by the doctor's assurance that there is nothing seriously wrong, surely the frightening feelings she experienced can't be as harmless as the doctor said? She has always been so healthy and now in her mid-twenties she is happily married with a toddler and a young baby. She feels there was no reason for her to have gone through such an overwhelming experience and is mortified at the thought of having made such a fool of herself in public.

By the time Mike collects her, Jane is almost back to her normal self. 'What came over you?' he asks. 'I was told you fainted in the street. You've never fainted in your life!'

'I felt faint,' Jane admits. 'But I didn't actually pass out. I was so frightened, my legs turned to jelly and I just sat down on the pavement. That's when someone sent for an ambulance – they thought I was having a heart attack. Surely anxiety couldn't have had such a devastating effect? Why did it happen? *What if it happens again?*'

Next day Jane visits her GP. 'Lots of people may have an anxiety or panic attack,' she is told as she is prescribed a week's supply of tranquillisers, given a pep talk and told to relax and stop worrying.

The family is reassuring, reminding her that she has recently got over a bad cold which hung around for a couple of weeks. 'You're just a bit run down,' her mother tells her. How comforting. A few days resting at home with her mother and sister helping with the children, and Jane feels she will be back to normal.

A week later Jane has almost forgotten her frightening experience in the High Street. She leaves the children with her mother while she and Mike visit the supermarket and do the weekend shopping. What a relief, she thinks . . . no unpleasant symptoms, everything is back to normal. She goes with her mother to buy clothes for the children. Nothing untoward happens and Jane feels confident enough to make the next trip to the supermarket on her own.

The supermarket is warm and bright; the usual crowd of weekend shoppers bustle about. Suddenly the lights seem to flicker, Jane's eyes are playing tricks and the noise of the people around her is overwhelming. It's happening again, she thinks, as she tries to fight the rising fear which is becoming difficult to control. Oblivious of the other shoppers she abandons her shopping trolley and escapes through the nearest checkout to get to the car park, where to her relief the frightening feelings subside almost immediately.

The way to stop these feelings recurring must be to avoid the supermarket altogether for the time being. Jane feels that the constant worrying is beginning to affect her in other ways and she feels on edge and jittery all the time. Shopping locally seems to be the answer, and all goes well at first until one day as she is walking along the street the dreaded feelings start building up once again. She feels unsafe and afraid – but what is she afraid of? Not of the shops nor the street, but of the feeling of fear itself.

Time to return to the GP. This time Jane breaks down and cries in the surgery as she tells him she is afraid she is going out of her mind.

A course of antidepressant drugs will help, the doctor tells her, but he will refer her to a psychologist for therapy – unfortunately there is a long waiting list and it could be several months before she can get the help she needs to overcome her panic attacks. In the meantime she should contact one of the self-help groups and learn to manage her recovery.

Perhaps you can identify with Jane and need to know what is the next step to managing your fears. You may not be suffering from panic attacks but have other deep-seated problems such as chronic anxiety; you may suffer from one or many phobias or some other nervous problem that you are desperate to overcome.

Where do you start? First of all you have to learn to face your fears and not be frightened by them. Fear of the fear is the shadow that hangs over you, and once you have mastered that fear you can then tackle the other problems. It won't be easy, but remember: if you had a broken leg you would have to face weeks of physiotherapy, often painful, before you could walk properly again.

Many anxious people cannot bear to read descriptions of symptoms, but you do not 'catch' feelings you read about, even if your imagination makes you feel uncomfortable. Keep reading and you will be surprised at your relief at knowing you are not alone or different from everyone else.

2

Understanding your nerves

Why I fear I know not; but yet as one deprived of
sense I fear all things.

Ovid

The old English word *faer* meant 'sudden danger'. Fear is what
we experience when something unpleasant or dangerous is
happening to us; without any conscious effort our body
immediately reacts by producing sensations which are often
as unpleasant as the cause. The heart beats faster, blood is
shifted from other areas of the body to the limb muscles and
to the brain, encouraging quick thinking and vigorous activity.
Adrenalin and related chemicals which are released into the
bloodstream provide additional strength, stamina and the
ability to respond rapidly. These chemicals help soldiers
to survive in battle, athletes to perform better and all
individuals to respond more effectively when faced with
dangerous situations.

There are people who actually enjoy these sensations,

finding them exciting and stimulating, and they frequently seek a career or hobby where there is an element of danger, indulging in hair-raising activities in the name of adventure, exploration or sport. (Think bungee-jumping, white-water rafting and even some of the gut-wrenching rides found in amusement parks.)

Most of us are ashamed to admit that we might be nervous or fearful, since courage has always been considered to be a superior virtue and from childhood we are told to be brave and not show our fears. There can be a backlash, though, because some children – particularly boys – are so conditioned to be 'brave' that they become over-confident, foolhardy and accident-prone.

Many of the world's great heroes killed in battle might have lived to fight another day if they had been less fearless and more cautious. At the Battle of Trafalgar, Lord Nelson insisted on wearing all his medals and decorations so that the enemy could identify and marvel at the bold British admiral . . . they made a great target for a French sniper, and the man who in his youth had remarked, 'Fear, what is that?' returned to his homeland pickled in a keg of brandy.

Our forebears had good reason to be fearful. In order to survive it was necessary for people to be continually on the alert for danger. Marauding tribes and dangerous animals on the prowl were a constant threat when you had only a club for a weapon and the sparse shelter of a cave to retreat into. When danger threatened, these people, their survival at risk, would be 'tensed up' and ready for action – to stand and fight or to run for their lives.

Over the centuries, as we have become more or less civilised, survival has become easier and most of the earlier dangers have disappeared. Of course, modern humanity has its problems – mainly of our own making – but apart from those people for whom danger is a normal way of life, either in their profession or for entertainment, most of us are fairly assured of our survival to a ripe old age, bar accident or illness. The danger response is not now a necessary daily part of our bodily functions, so when it does occur it is likely to have longer-lasting disturbing effects. The cave people, victorious in battle or having escaped from a woolly mammoth or a sabre-tooth tiger for the umpteenth time, would relax and sleep by the fire, forgetting their nerve-racking experience until the next time. Nowadays, the emotional consequences of a bad shock or accident will persist for much longer, and being unused to such experiences we resent the effect they have on our well-being.

A certain amount of fear is healthy and it prevents us from risking ourselves in dangerous situations. There are, however, many of us who because of our personalities are more prone to fear than others. We can all understand being terrified when confronted with a dangerous situation, though in these days, apart from being attacked by a mugger or injured in a car accident, life isn't all that dangerous. If we are faced with a life-threatening situation, however, the 'flight or fight' response that our cave people experienced is perfectly normal. In fact, it is imperative that our automatic system goes into overdrive in order that we may tackle the emergency or retreat from the scene as quickly as possible.

But sometimes we get the wrong signals. A sudden surge of fear, even when no danger exists, causes bodily changes. Adrenalin pours into the system, the body prepares itself for action . . . but no action follows. If the nervous energy could be discharged, the body would settle down. But when this does not happen there is physiological confusion. I'm sure you recognise the sensations: racing heart, dry mouth, clammy hands, overbreathing, dizziness, a 'tight band round the head', vision disturbance, a 'lump' in the throat and buzzing in the ears. The feelings build up until they seem unbearable and the sufferer, clinging to the nearest static object to support her 'jelly legs', thinks, 'I can't stand it. My system won't take any more. I'll have a heart attack, a stroke, a burst blood vessel. I'll drop down dead, I know I will . . .'

This is the classic description of a panic attack as experienced by Jane in the previous chapter. Unfortunately the word 'panic' suggests a loss of control resulting in the person screaming and running round in circles. The usual panic attack sufferer does not behave like this. She (or he) feels overcome by feelings of acute fear, but most shrink at the thought of drawing attention to themselves. The struggle to appear calm increases the tension and terror as they fight to conceal their distress. The feelings build up until they seem unbearable and the sufferer, clinging to the nearest static object for support, waits for some dreadful climax. There is no climax. The sensations can only reach a certain level and then they subside.

This does not mean that there are no after-effects of such an experience; a severe panic attack can leave you in a highly sensitised state, weak and exhausted, but it cannot damage you, either physically or mentally.

Anxiety

My apprehensions come in crowds;
I dread the rustling of the grass;
The very shadows of the clouds
Have power to shake me as they pass.

William Wordsworth,
The Affliction of Margaret

Wordsworth's Margaret suffered from a problem with which many of us can identify today. He describes a general anxiety disorder, a disproportionate sense of fear and apprehension induced without good reason. Millions of people in the world go through life feeling that there is something terribly wrong with them because of the constant anxiety that pervades their lives. It may be a state of galloping panic, it may be a continuous feeling of uncertainty and conviction that something is not quite right.

Anxiety is the permanent companion of so many of us. The Latin word *anxius* means to press tightly or to strangle; the dictionary defines 'anxiety' as 'a state of chronic apprehension'. Men and women are blessed – some may say cursed – with imagination; they can project their thoughts into the future and anticipate what *might* happen rather than what actually *will* happen . . . and what misery this can cause. Too often anxiety develops into a chronic condition where the sufferer is afraid of the anxiety itself and is then caught in a vicious circle which is difficult to break.

Some people are naturally timid, going through life trying to avoid confrontations that they feel might upset their equilibrium. Rude behaviour from a stranger or a family row will upset them for days and they will avoid arguments at all costs. It is now accepted that many of us are born with a predisposition towards anxiety; others, as we shall see later in this book, may become oversensitised as the result of some traumatic event, psychological or physiological, and find that they cannot cope with the stresses of everyday life.

In their highly sensitised state these people may experience chronic, nagging anxiety which can disrupt their lifestyles or, in more severe cases, become overwhelmed by sudden devastating attacks of acute anxiety, commonly called panic attacks.

Many people will experience a panic attack at some time in their lives. The after-effects of a serious illness, seeing or being involved in an accident, or experiencing some other traumatic event may result in a one-off panic attack – and that's understandable. Almost everyone at some time feels sick, weak, faint or over-anxious, but these feelings are soon shaken off and we are reassured because we know there was a reason for them. However, there are some people who can experience four or more panic attacks every month without any obvious reason, and this is when the anticipatory anxiety builds up . . . the 'what if?' syndrome. What if I have a panic attack at work? . . . at school? . . . in the cinema? *Anywhere*? Now the sufferer is faced with the most crippling phobia of them all: fear of fear itself. We know this as agoraphobia. For many years agoraphobia was understood to be a fear of open spaces, but you will see that this was a misnomer.

Though sufferers have often been unwilling to admit to being agoraphobic, the condition has been recognised for a long time. Richard Burton wrote in 1621 of:

> one that durst not walk alone from home for fear he should swoon or die . . . if he be in a throng, middle of a church or multitude, where he may not well go out, though he sit at ease he is so misaffected.

3

Agoraphobia

Nothing is terrible except fear itself.
Francis Bacon

Constant panic attacks become 'panic disorder' and, as the sufferer knows, they can strike at any time and in any situation. Because they usually happen away from the safety of the home, the term 'agoraphobia' was used in the past to signify a fear of open spaces.

The Greeks had the correct definition – *agora*, the market place or place of assembly, and *phobos*, terror or flight. They understood the panic-stricken need to escape from a situation – wherever it was, indoors or outside – when the feelings of fear became overwhelming

Those who have not experienced this problem naturally find it difficult to comprehend the extent of the suffering it causes. It is a condition that defies easy description, for these days the word 'agoraphobia' is used as a collective term for a number of unpleasant sensations which can, if allowed, wreck the life of the sufferer, but which appear to bear little relation

13

to the original definition: fear of open spaces. Fear is there, certainly, but fear of what? Not of the great outdoors, the shopping centre, the motorway – but fear of the terrifying irrational feeling of anxiety escalating to panic which for no apparent reason can overwhelm the victim. One person may well experience these feelings in a shopping centre, another in an open field, another on a bus or in church. Yet another sufferer may be affected in each one of these situations, but what we have to understand is that it is not the 'place of assembly' – the theatre or the supermarket – that is the object of the phobia; these become places to be avoided because they are the settings associated with the fear.

When panic strikes, the overwhelming need is to escape. If you are out in the open you must get under cover; if you are in a confined space you look round for an exit. You must get away from the people milling about you, must escape from the noise, the silence, the bright lights, the darkness. There are so many things to dread and all of them contradict each other. No wonder the sufferer is confused when told that agoraphobia is the problem when she feels just as panic-stricken in a lift or hemmed in by a crowd. Isn't this *claustrophobia*?

The definitions of the two states may appear to be contradictory, but agoraphobia and claustrophobia both apply to a state of anxiety which manifests itself in certain situations, causing feelings of terror and a need to escape from and avoid these situations.

Trapped! Inside or out, the feelings are the same. Agoraphobia may begin when a panic attack strikes in a specific situation. The situation itself becomes the focus of the fear as the subject expects a repetition of the original panic attack and, anticipating it, involuntarily triggers it off.

Judith: Each day on my way to work I have to pass a high fence about a hundred yards long. On the other side of the road is a church with a very tall steeple, which soars into the sky. I try to avoid looking up at it as I begin to feel dizzy and slightly sick, and I walk along beside the fence which appears to go on for ever. I feel more and more disorientated. If I break into a run my heart starts to race and I begin to sweat.

How crazy to be afraid of a stretch of road! I cannot avoid it as it is the only approach to the local train station and I must get to the city centre to my office. I have seriously thought of giving up my job because I cannot face this daily ordeal for much longer.

The agoraphobic's dilemma is that if she experiences these feelings in certain places, she will avoid these places in order to avert the panic; but with sensations of anxiety always present she then begins to worry about other situations. She expects the panic to occur – so it does, almost as though her mind has an 'on' switch which operates whenever she thinks about the dreaded spot. The trouble is that she does not know how to operate the 'off' switch, so she retreats to safety – only soon nowhere is safe. If she is really unlucky she will feel that the only place to avoid panic is behind her own front door; but even then, if the habit of switching on fear has become established, the security of her home may not protect her from the dreaded attacks.

Some long-term agoraphobics may not be able to recall the last time they experienced a full-blown panic attack but, trapped by the *fear of fear*, they are not prepared to risk facing a dreaded situation – just in case.

Who suffers from agoraphobia?

It is difficult to estimate the number of agoraphobics in the UK. We really have no idea how many there are as the number of people receiving treatment is a very small proportion of the whole, but best estimates are that it varies between three and five million.

At one end of the scale are those whose phobia affects their lifestyle totally, even to the extent of them becoming housebound, while at the other end there is an army of women and men whose symptoms are mildly disturbing but manageable, who would never dream of admitting to such problems and would certainly not seek treatment for what they would probably describe as a 'nuisance'.

As the official number of agoraphobics is based on the number receiving treatment it is obvious that this is quite irrelevant.

Men suffer too

In the early days of *The Open Door* (TOD) it was thought that as many as 90 per cent of agoraphobics were women. Now it is recognised as being around 75 per cent.

In the 1960s when I started TOD all our publicity was through women's magazines, with articles such as 'A prisoner in her own home', accompanied by photographs of a middle-aged woman peering anxiously through her net curtains. Programmes such as *Woman's Hour* featured such women, and all the agony aunts in the women's magazines reassured sufferers from panic attacks and agoraphobia, referring them to TOD and the other phobia organisations then springing up. No one seemed concerned about any men who might be experiencing the same problems until the

1970s, when the media began to acknowledge this.

At last, newspapers, radio and TV featured male agoraphobics and how their lives were affected by the condition. At once the phobia organisations began to hear from more and more men, many of them in their early twenties, which was a surprise to some of us. Until then, agoraphobia had been assumed to be a female disorder.

History: fact and fiction

Phobias are not a phenomenon of contemporary life; through the ages people have suffered from a variety of phobias, but it is interesting to find that there are few historical references to women being affected. This does not mean that women did not suffer from them, but probably reflects the sexist bias that only events happening to men were worth recording!

Apparently there was no shame attached to a man admitting to a specific phobia, but when agoraphobia, with its background of sudden panic attacks, became recognised, it quickly came to be considered a woman's problem. Described as the housebound housewife's complaint or the 'empty nest syndrome', it was linked with menopausal women whose children had left home. Even more alarming, until recent years agoraphobia was known as the 'Latent Prostitute Syndrome' and still is in some Scandinavian countries. This assumes that these women are afraid that unmanageable sexual urges might cause them to attack a man in the street. Therefore it is safer for them to stay indoors away from temptation!

It is hardly surprising that agoraphobic men disliked being identified as suffering from the condition as they battled on, determined to lead as normal a life as possible. Many men have a horror of anyone knowing they are agoraphobic, as there is often a definite possibility of jobs being at risk and careers ruined if their 'weakness' is exposed. At one time there were a number of well-known men in *The Open Door* – television and other media personalities, an eminent lawyer, several doctors and even a Member of Parliament. The late Roy Plomley, famous for his programme *Desert Island Discs*, admitted (privately) that he could imagine nothing more traumatic than being stranded on an island with no possibility of escape. Roy's agoraphobia was so bad that his wife had to drive him to and from the BBC; he couldn't travel on his own by public transport, nor could he drive his car alone.

There are, of course, a few recorded incidences of male agoraphobics, including – of all people – Sigmund Freud, who for several years had a fear of travelling and became so anxious that he would arrive at a station an hour before his train was due to leave.

Charles Darwin, after sailing with the *Beagle*, gathering material for *The Origin of Species*, suffered from panic attacks and agoraphobia after the death of his young daughter.

A professor of English at Cambridge suffered from agoraphobia for forty-eight years, managing to hide this from colleagues and students and never seeking medical help. Only his family and close friends knew of his condition, though it may well have been noticed by others that the only way he could cross the college quadrangle was by sidling around the sides with his back to the wall.

Women, of course, always accepted in earlier times to have a more delicate constitution, were not so reticent about admitting to nervous problems. There are many examples during the last hundred years or so of women who were quite possibly suffering from what we would now recognise as agoraphobia. Shock, anxiety, frustration and physical ill health often lie behind the development of agoraphobic symptoms. How many swooning Victorian matrons languished on their daybeds? How many wilting maidens suffered fits of 'vapours' or slipped into a decline that might today be recognised as agoraphobia?

In later life, Florence Nightingale, with no physical outlet for her tremendous nervous energy, became housebound and was a semi-invalid for many years. After the shock of Prince Albert's death, Queen Victoria retreated from public life, unable to face her subjects *en masse*. Elizabeth Barrett was confined to her couch with physical symptoms which miraculously improved after Robert Browning whisked her off to Italy and married her. Retrospectively we can only guess, but each of these ladies displayed classic agoraphobic tendencies. Even in fiction there is Charles Dickens' Miss Havisham in *Great Expectations*, housebound since being jilted on her wedding day.

Not *all* agoraphobia sufferers experience constant panic attacks. Some people, women in particular, may become housebound for a variety of reasons, resulting in a loss of confidence and unwillingness to leave the house. The longer this lasts, the more nervous the subject becomes as the outside world appears hostile and threatening. If she is persuaded to go further than her base she may well experience rising anxiety, leading to a full-blown panic attack.

Many agoraphobics are free from their fear when driving because the family car can feel like an extension of the home; like a snail or a tortoise, these sufferers would like to carry with them a permanent shell into which they can retreat at any time.

Unfortunately, agoraphobia/driving phobia seems to be on the increase, among both men and women. On motorways in particular, nervous feelings begin to build up when surrounded by heavy trucks belting along, spraying smaller cars with water, mud and dust. It might be ten miles to the next turn-off, time to let anxiety build up until the driver finds the tension unbearable. He cannot stop, and feels as though he is whirling into space and there is no escape.

Ken: Driving along the motorway at around sixty miles an hour, I thought I must have been in an accident and died, the sensation was so weird and 'out of this world'. After the first flash of fear I managed to drive on to the hard shoulder and pull up. By that time I was shaking violently, sweat was pouring from me and I felt as though a great weight was pressing on me, stopping me from breathing. It was no accident, I realised, but by then I was convinced I was having a heart attack. There was no way I could get out of the car to get help; I just sat there trying to make sense out of the totally unreal feelings. After some five minutes things began to get back to normal and I nervously started the car, creeping along cautiously, hoping I would reach the next exit safely. Once off the motorway I felt slightly better and eventually got home.

Unfortunately this has happened a couple of times since. I am a professional man in my forties and consider myself pretty well-balanced. These episodes have shaken me badly; I now wait for the next attack to hit me and am beginning to feel that somehow I am going to have to avoid motorways altogether.

Travelling is the agoraphobic's worst nightmare, particularly if he has to use public transport. Mingling with fellow travellers, waiting interminably for a bus or train while the anxiety grows, having to stand because there are no available seats – these are all situations which the sufferer dreads, believing that he is not going to survive without making an exhibition of himself.

Jo (sixteen): I have to take two buses and walk half a mile to school each day. Several of us travel together but I couldn't manage on my own. I live in dread that my friends might be ill or not coming to school that day for some reason. It is the walk that I feel I can't face. I dream about it most nights and see myself losing control, fainting or screaming. I never have fainted but the thought hangs over me like a dark cloud.

My doctor says I have agoraphobia and has put me on a waiting list for treatment at the hospital. He was a bit vague about what sort of therapy I will need and I am now very worried because I don't know what to expect. I've read about electro-convulsive therapy: I don't think I could face that. My imagination is working overtime filling me with fear and dread.

Although Jo's agoraphobia is fairly mild it could get worse if she doesn't have some help now. She could probably get help from one of the phobia organisations but as she is on a hospital waiting list it is important for her to know what to expect. *Not* ECT, for a start. One of the reasons so many agoraphobics refused to seek treatment in the past was that they knew the condition was often treated by electro-convulsive therapy. Forty years ago, when it was assumed that agoraphobia was automatically linked with depression, many people underwent shock treatment for something they did not suffer from – it did nothing for their phobia. Depressed? Of course they were depressed: they were faced with the possibility of becoming permanently housebound and no one could explain to them exactly what was the matter. In the majority of cases the depression was caused by the agoraphobia, not vice versa.

There is a school of thought which feels that the cause of

agoraphobia must be identified before the patient can be helped through analysis and psychotherapy, and it is obvious that if someone is seriously disturbed, psychotherapy will be a vital part of their treatment. However, most agoraphobics can pinpoint the onset of their condition to a time following a major upset in their lives.

There is no need to look for hidden origins to phobias and obsessions. They do not point to dark, unconscious secrets which have to be uncovered for treatment to succeed. The anxieties can be cleared by working on the assumption that the sufferer needs to get used to the situation which troubles him, without any need to reconstruct his personality.

Isaac Marks, *Living with Fear*

Those of us who have emerged from the shadow of agoraphobia know that there is only one way to tackle it, and that is by exposure to the situations which you feel you cannot face – exposure to the situation *and* exposure to the unpleasant symptoms. Agoraphobics are inclined to judge their progress on their ability not to feel panic. Two or three panic-free trips to the supermarket; they are doing really well. Then on the next occasion the old frightening feelings come flooding back and it's back to square one again.

Face the fear. Enter into the phobic situation. Sounds simple and easy to do, but it can seem an insurmountable task for the agoraphobic. The most traumatic approach is known as *flooding*, where the patient is exposed to her most dreaded situation and encouraged to remain within it, experiencing the worst sensations that her phobia can produce, facing the panic feelings and the distress that follows until the peak is past and the symptoms gradually evaporate. This might take a few minutes, or it might take an hour or two, but the important point is that the sufferer stands her ground until the anxiety starts to lessen, and has to be prepared to remain until it does.

The patient's fear is that her system cannot tolerate the acute phase of a panic attack, that there must be some terrible climax which will prove fatal. This is not so; when the panic feelings reach a peak there is only one way they can go – down. They will gradually subside and the sufferer will find herself sick and shaky but still in one piece ... and a step nearer recovery.

There is no doubt that such an experience is more exhausting than exhilarating, but it cannot be denied that *if she is well prepared by her therapist and has the motivation and the courage to co-operate, this can be the fastest way to overcome agoraphobia.*

Systematic desensitisation was popular in the 1970s as this was a more acceptable form of therapy for the patients. It involved learning to relax completely before visualising the phobic situations that the agoraphobic most feared. Learning to curb her out-of-control imagination was difficult, but the therapist would then guide her to the next stage – actually going to these places and finding that she could tolerate them *without experiencing a panic attack.*

This approach was very time-consuming for the therapist and unrealistic for the patient who, happily acclimatising herself to the phobic situations, was unprepared when a panic attack did materialise, didn't know how to cope with it and became disillusioned with the treatment.

These days the patient is instructed to take a different view of her phobia, changing her negative attitude towards the problem ('*I know I shall have a panic attack*') and telling herself instead, '*I shall probably feel panicky but I am no longer*

*frightened by the thought of this as I understand how to over-
come it.'*

Instead of the flooding approach, where the agoraphobic
was plunged into her worst nightmare and forced to endure
the panic until it peaked then subsided, she is now instructed
by her therapist to take it a step at a time.

She is told to 'construct a hierarchy' – making a list of her
phobic situations ranging from the very mild to the most
alarming. Listing them from one to ten, she will then proceed
up the scale, learning to tolerate each one before progressing
to one she finds more difficult.

The object of the exercise is not to try and avoid a panic
attack but to actively encourage it to do its worst. Knowing
that it is not going to damage her in any way, the agoraphobic
goes through the experience, emerging at the end unscathed.
Unlike the flooding technique the process is gradual, and the
patient does not have to tackle her worst fears until she is well
prepared.

In Chapter 18 of this book we will see how to apply
the self-help approach using this technique. I would encourage you to join one of the phobia organisations who have
experience in helping sufferers in both one-to-one and group
situations.

PAX newsletters are full of enthusiastic reports from
recovering members.

Penny (thirty): I was never completely housebound but was
heading that way. My GP prescribed Seroxat, and although
it took several weeks before I noticed any effect it has been
extremely helpful. I was told by my GP that I also needed
to see a cognitive behavioural therapist as I could not rely
on drugs for ever and must learn how to manage panic
attacks if they returned. I found this a rather depressing

outlook. Eventually I did see a behaviourist, by which time my GP had weaned me off Seroxat, encouraging me to try and do without it.

Unfortunately the panic attacks returned. It had been so easy to live a normal, panic-free life and I rather resented finding myself back to square one. I had to learn to tolerate the panics – though it took several attempts to get through the first occasions when I had to stand *outside* the supermarket. I didn't know it at the time, but my husband was hovering about, out of my sight. He wasn't convinced that I wasn't going to react badly, collapse or burst into tears. The therapist wasn't too pleased when he found out and Richard was told quite firmly that he was to keep right away and let me work towards recovery on my own, without him fussing around me.

I realised how much I had depended on Richard's support in the past, but it was pointed out to both of us that his attitude was holding me back.

After four months I can now shop in the supermarket on my own. I still dread the panic attacks but am learning to tolerate them. My next step is a train journey – alone. I would feel happier if the trains were more reliable, as they are inclined to stop sometimes for fifteen minutes between stations. If this happens I shall look on this as an opportunity to put into practice all I have been taught about going through panic.

Many people have written to me who are having professional help and making progress with their recovery, and remind me about the late Dr Claire Weekes. In the 1960s her books helped thousands, and her advice is as appropriate today as it was forty years ago when *Self Help for Your Nerves* was the most requested book in libraries all over the world.

William wrote to the PAX newsletter:

I am a man of thirty-one and a recovered agoraphobic (note 'recovered', not 'recovering'). I have had six months of treatment – behavioural therapy at my local hospital – and I am for ever grateful to those who have helped me tackle my fears and overcome them.

I also attribute much of my present happy state to Claire Weekes, the Australian doctor whose books helped me through the worst time in my life when suffering constant panic attacks. I had to be persuaded by my mother to look at these books – I thought they were just for neurotic women.

Dr Weekes teaches four concepts of fear:

Face fear – do not run away.
Accept fear – do not fight it.
Float through fear – do not run away.
Let time pass – do not be impatient.

I would urge fellow PAX members to read *Self Help for Your Nerves*.

4

Social phobia

Other people are quite dreadful. The only possible society is oneself.

Oscar Wilde

'A cure for shyness!' Newspaper headlines in the late 1990s were quickly taken up by the programme *This Morning* when Richard Madeley and Judy Finnegan told the nation that this new drug would transform the lives of people who suffered from devastating shyness. In fact, this drug – Seroxat (Paroxetine), an antidepressant – was not new. For several years it had been prescribed for depression, panic attacks and agoraphobia, and a large number of PAX members were finding it very helpful towards overcoming their problems. Recently, though, Seroxat had been hailed as the new treatment for social phobias and acute shyness.

This Morning's presenters announced that they would hand out supplies of the drug to volunteers, who would be asked to try it out 'for a few days' and then report back to the programme, hopefully to tell viewers that their shyness had disappeared and that they were able to enjoy a full social life once more.

Fortunately, some concerned doctors and some of us involved in the phobia organisations managed to stop this irresponsible experiment before it got under way. Can you imagine the hopes raised and then dashed to the ground? Of course, the drug has been of great help to thousands with anxiety problems, but it takes a good three weeks to act and it needs to be prescribed by a doctor or psychiatrist, preferably in conjunction with further therapy.

What a fuss to make about being shy, you might think. After all, thousands and thousands of people suffer from shyness and a lack of self-confidence. Surely it is a matter of facing up to life and tackling problems, something that would automatically improve with maturity?

Social phobia is a growing problem which affects equal numbers of men and women, unlike agoraphobia, which is a condition more often attributed to women, though there is a considerable overlap between social phobia and agoraphobia.

The agoraphobia sufferer has a need to escape to safety. She may be in a crowd of people, she may be alone in her phobic situation, but she feels trapped by her inability to detach herself quickly from the place where she is uncomfortable and escape to her home or somewhere where she feels safe.

The person who suffers from social phobia does not have the same need to escape from a situation; it is other people he finds threatening. He cannot bear to be looked at, to have his body space invaded, to be touched, even inadvertently. Some sufferers find it physically impossible to touch or be touched by anyone other than members of their own immediate family.

Social phobics feel they are under scrutiny all the time; they imagine that all eyes are upon them and experience symptoms of acute anxiety, displaying outward signs of distress such as blushing, sweating and hyperventilating which they are sure everyone notices and despises them for. They are afraid of drawing attention to themselves, of being embarrassed by making a mistake or making fools of themselves. At the root of their shame is a fear of losing control in some way or not being able to continue what they are doing while they are being watched.

Social phobics often find themselves unable to relate to other people on any sort of personal level. They may have difficulty in expressing their emotions and feel that they cannot get close to others physically or emotionally; often, they are children who have had an over-protected upbringing, have not developed a sense of independence and are therefore unable to function adequately in an adult social world.

Dr Alan Wade, a GP from Clydebank, became aware of the condition through his interest in phobias and panic attacks.

'Sufferers grossly underachieve,' he says. 'They often don't earn as much as the average person and favour solitary jobs where they can avoid scrutiny. They may even choose to be unemployed because they can't face going out. They are prone to depression and other disorders such as agoraphobia, which has similar symptoms.'

These phobias do not evoke much sympathy in those who have never experienced them. On the whole they seem trivial and sufferers do their best to hide them, feeling that they might be laughed at. Walking past a line of people standing at a bank counter, writing a cheque, speaking in front of a class – such simple actions for most of us, but agonising for many social phobia sufferers.

How can a visit to the bank be as traumatic as a visit to the dentist? It is the way that a phobic person's mind works –

always jumping ahead, expecting the worst. One member of PAX explains his fear of his bank and the thoughts that run through his mind.

> There are a lot of people waiting, I feel trapped already. I should have checked how much there is in my account. Supposing there isn't enough to cover this cheque? Why is the bank clerk looking at me in that funny way? What is the computer telling her? Why has she walked away? Everyone is looking at me.

By this time he can hardly take his money because his hand is shaking so much.

Another PAX member, this time a woman, wrote:

> I cannot bear to be looked at. I am afraid I might do something silly, make a fool of myself, make a mistake or lose control in some way. More than anything I am afraid of anyone KNOWING I'm afraid.

Again, the problem is the need to escape before she commits the dreadful crime of drawing attention to herself. As we see, this is closely linked to the agoraphobic state. Avoiding social situations means that she may become housebound, but unlike the agoraphobic who can find sanctuary from her fears in her home, the social phobic finds that her problems follow her indoors.

To this person, the arrival of an unexpected caller can be a disaster. The sound of the doorbell, a knock on the door, sets off warning signals. Who is it? Why are they here? What do they want? These thoughts flash through her mind as she ducks into a corner where she cannot be seen. Her heart races, her mouth dries up as she feels the situation is getting out of hand and she won't be able to cope. The only thing to do is to stay hidden until they go away. Unfortunately there are times when visitors must be faced.

Even the sound of the telephone can be as alarming as the unexpected caller. When someone is hypersensitive the sudden sound can make them jump and their heart beat faster. Who is on the other end of the line? When fear has dried your mouth it is difficult to speak and you worry about what the caller might think. Will you be able to answer their questions, can you make an excuse to put the phone down? You have to answer it because it may be a member of your family in trouble or some other emergency.

Another problem the social phobic has is eating in public, particularly in a restaurant or at an important social function, though some people may find the experience of eating with just a couple of friends or even members of the family equally distressing.

Rose, aged twenty-two, had an unfortunate experience: when lunching with a group of old school friends, she had to leave the table, feeling unwell and nauseous.

I could not rejoin them because the feelings just overwhelmed me again, and although my friends were sympathetic I felt ashamed and embarrassed. Since that time I have felt unable to eat in front of other people. As I am to be married in six months' time the thought of the wedding reception is with me the whole time and I live in dread of the occasion.

I make no excuses for including all these examples of social phobia. I feel it is important that people understand just how life-disrupting this problem can be for the sufferer.

Blushing is a major problem for those who feel the need to hide their fears from other people. A scarlet face is impossible to conceal and inevitably draws attention to the blusher and comments from their companions.

Martin: I have been a social phobic since I was a child of ten years old. Even before this age I had other phobias and terrible anxiety. This phobia has ruined my whole life. The main symptom is a terrible fear of blushing, which happens instantly in nearly every social situation. The way I deal with these situations may sound pitiful to others who can't possibly imagine how it feels.

At the age of eleven in school I used to sit always against a wall so that one side of my face would be covered. Nobody could see that side because of the wall. Then I would rest my elbow on the desk and cover my other cheek by resting it in my hand. I would literally be trying to hide my face from everyone. I would avoid any group situation and I used to spend hours walking the playing fields on my own, avoiding contact with anyone.

Other ways I would try to deal with this phobia were to pretend I had a cold or flu and whenever someone spoke to me I would take my handkerchief and blow my nose (another way of hiding my face). At other times I have burned my face on purpose with a sun lamp so that no one could see when I was blushing. I was teased and ridiculed in school, even by my so-called friends.

I can still recall the terrible anxiety that I felt from 9.00 till 3.45 every day of the week. However, it didn't end there because the phobia applied to absolutely everybody, so when I got home I couldn't eat with my parents. I would take my food on a tray to the darkest room in the house to eat it, as I was ashamed of blushing in front of my family, and unfortunately today at the age of thirty-five I still am.

Because of PAX I have been able to face up to the problem and seek help at last. Though I have a long way to go I am determined to overcome this, having tackled the first obstacle – learning that *it doesn't matter*.

Allison is in her late twenties:

I am a social phobic. My panic attacks started when I was at secondary school. I was always blushing from an early age but hadn't actually experienced panic attacks until I was directly asked questions in a classroom or had to give presentations. Simply walking into someone I knew would leave me a mess. After leaving school I chose a university course that avoided presentations and tutorials, for I knew that if I had to talk to a group of people my panic attacks would be unbearable.

However, after I arrived at university I found the course had changed and tutorials and presentations were compulsory. I managed to get away with attending the minimum of tutorials or being signed off sick, but every presentation I had to do would end in a severe panic attack, even after four years. Sometimes the panic attacks would last up to an hour or more, and the embarrassment and shame lasted for a year afterwards. Sometimes I would get so drunk the night before that I would still knowingly be drunk while doing the presentation the next morning . . . the alcohol helped me to avoid a panic attack.

After leaving university I worked in various jobs where I could avoid any position of responsibility and confrontation with others, although tasks such as typing, writing or answering the phone in front of anybody would leave me shaking, flushed, faint, having palpitations and with a numb left arm for anything up to an hour afterwards. If anyone came to talk to me and looked me in the eye, the same things would happen. I could not even carry a cup of tea without having to sit down if I knew someone was watching.

Socially I could not eat in public without severe tremors – or even lift a glass to my mouth in front of anyone. I could not sit at a table with people looking or talking to me without blushing, which would lead to panic attacks. I could not take hold of salt or pepper pots without shaking, or even sign my cheques or Switch receipts in shops. All these things became impossible and I avoided them at all costs – unless, of course, I was drunk first, knowing that the next day the symptoms would then be much worse! If ever I walked into someone I knew, I would have a panic attack when they saw me and so I avoided going out. If anyone stared at me on the tube I would have an attack, and if I was standing up I would feel I was going to pass out, blinded with dizziness and acute panic.

This has been my life for the last five years, and each new counsellor I got I prayed would help – but to no avail. I have had cognitive behaviour therapy, hypnotherapy and done a lot of work myself to try and solve the problem. Nothing worked, much to the dismay of *all* my counsellors, who knew that I knew what they were going to say next!

So I ended up severely depressed whereas I had not been depressed before. I was ashamed to go to work where everyone felt sorry for me and I left my job. I was scared to go out in public places where I knew I'd meet someone I knew, and as my depression worsened I couldn't face *any* public place. Sometimes when I was on my own I also suffered – if I got a piece of food stuck in my throat, if I thought I had left the gas cooker on, if I thought I might be late for something – so it was not just social situations that instigated the panic. Carrying around an enormous and unbearable weight from my throat to my stomach became my life, until I finally accepted the fact that I would have to take medication as I couldn't continue like this.

I was loath to take drugs but took my doctor's advice and am now on an antidepressant which took some weeks to work, but I persisted. This drug has had some side-effects but I am no longer suicidal. The weight has lifted; I can get out of bed, can work and not panic and I can go out in public. Although nobody believes me I would definitely not be here today if it was not for this drug.

Many social phobic young people find school life very difficult. They may be brilliant scholars but they are struggling with their fears of people and find it difficult to settle in school and make the most of their academic talents.

An adolescent social phobic is in a sorry plight, particularly if he also develops agoraphobia, which often happens, causing him to become housebound. Lack of contact with his peers exacerbates the condition and may result in a retreat into daydreams and fantasies, avoiding contact with the real world outside his home and inevitably losing touch with other people. A girl may hope for a romantic hero to arrive at her front door and sweep her off her feet, though she certainly would not be able to cope if he wanted to take her away from the safety of home.

It is especially difficult to persuade adolescents to take part in a treatment programme, as recovery would mean having to face up to the realities of normal everyday life.

Some older women who have become housebound may focus all their emotions on to a well-known celebrity – often an actor or a pop singer, and often dead (safer). Recently there was a television documentary about a woman who was in love with Elvis Presley, and her restricted life revolved around the singer, his recordings and a mountain of other memorabilia.

It is not only in the Western world that social phobia is a problem. In Japan, 1.2 million young people, 75 per cent of them boys and young men, suffer from severe social phobia known as *hikikomori*. They become completely isolated in their bedrooms, refusing to see or speak to anyone, including their own parents. Their families are so devastatingly embarrassed and ashamed that they keep it a secret and virtually isolate themselves. Because of their embarrassment the condition is only just becoming recognised, and at last counsellors are being trained to help the sufferers and the rest of their family.

It is suggested that the problem arises because of the huge pressures young people are under to succeed at school. They often start by developing school phobia and agoraphobia as they begin to avoid school. Severe social phobia develops from there, and the sufferer retreats from the outside world altogether.

This state of affairs wouldn't arise in Great Britain as therapy is available, although the waiting lists may be long. In the meantime, the phobia organisations can offer advice and practical help.

5

My story

I am quite myself again.
A. E. Housman

Panic attacks and agoraphobia were part of my life from childhood until my mid-twenties. My mother was agoraphobic and at one time was housebound for two years. I didn't even notice this, mainly because my brother and I, and later on our sister, were brought up by a nanny. We had a very happy childhood and a good social life, but I was a nervous child with an over-active imagination. I was happiest when retreating into a fantasy world and weaving stories to entertain my siblings and my friends.

One day I was enjoying my weekly ballet lesson. My mother sat with her friends and smiled encouragingly every time I caught her eye. As the winter afternoon was bleak and dark, someone switched on the lights, and suddenly from being a carefree child I became a nervous wreck for no apparent reason. The noise of the music was overwhelming, the lights were too bright and everything around me seemed unreal. I ran to my mother for reassurance, and after I had calmed down we went home and the family doctor was summoned. It was decided that I was suffering from a reaction to a tonsil operation I had had a few weeks earlier.

These days, I suppose this would have been diagnosed as a panic attack caused by post-traumatic stress, and certainly the experience had been particularly stressful. In the 1930s there was no such thing as a pre-operative sedative; I was wheeled straight into the operating theatre and, amid the frightening sight of surgical instruments and gowned adults, was held down while the rubber mask was placed over my face. I fought against the horrible smell of the gas, screaming with fright as the anaesthetic took effect. I can still remember vividly the sensation of falling and the blackness overcoming me while disembodied voices alternately soothed and scolded me.

Two weeks in hospital did not unduly disturb me and I didn't appear to have any after-effects. In fact, I soon forgot the ordeal and didn't worry abut it until the panic attack when I was dancing.

I never did go back to ballet lessons. I had a few mild panic attacks and felt generally jumpy but my mother reassured me and said the nerves were just something one had to put up with.

Some time later I had to visit the dentist. This was a regular occurrence and did not bother me until I saw the family doctor in the surgery and knew what that meant . . . *gas*. I fled from the surgery, out of the front door and along the road, pursued by several adults.

I was coaxed into having gas as a tooth had to come out, and although the experience wasn't too bad I convinced myself that my 'funny' feelings were similar to 'going under' the anaesthetic. This conviction stayed with me and severe dental phobia developed, soon joined by general fears of hospitals and doctors, fears which were to stay with me for the next twenty years and were joined by many others.

War was looming and we moved to the country. Sometimes at school I would experience fluttery feelings of anxiety, but being fairly stoical I put up with them. After all, my mother had assured me that they couldn't hurt me.

Unfortunately my all too vivid imagination was getting out of control, and as more and more phobias became part of my life I would go out of my way to avoid anything that might upset me. Apart from medical and dental phobias I had a horror of skeletons, people with any deformity, being blind-folded, hanging upside down (how I hated PE lessons), tunnels, travelling any distance, sleeping away from home, nose-bleeds, abstract thoughts, infinity, cemeteries, clouds, darkness, silence, thunderstorms – and tidal waves! I knew I would never see a tidal wave but the thought was disturbing.

The list was almost endless. There seemed to be so many upsetting things to cope with that I was only really happy in the fantasy world into which I slipped at every available opportunity.

School was becoming a problem. Morning assembly became an ordeal which had to be faced every day, but the dread of it was with me every waking moment. Most nights were disturbed by troubled dreams, and at breakfast I would feel sick and tearful, filled with worry about the coming day. The journey to school involved a long walk, a bus ride and another walk. This itself was becoming more and more difficult as panic was always just below the surface, waiting to strike if I allowed myself to stop and think. I became addicted to daydreaming to get away from the situation, pretending to be another more glamorous person triumphing over difficult and heroic situations. In my fantasy world, *I* was in control.

When filing into the school hall for assembly, my first thought was always what the hymn was for that day and how many verses it ran to. Up to three was bearable but any more and the panic would well up, making me feel sick, dizzy and unsteady. My great dread was that I might faint, though I never did. As things got worse I frequently had to slip out of the hall with the excuse that I felt unwell. There was no point in trying to explain further, I'd tried that and nobody understood.

Then sitting through lessons became difficult, and I was trying to avoid assembly by arriving late to school almost every day. The atmosphere that I had once enjoyed was becoming unbearable: too many people, too much noise – my mind felt overloaded and I could not concentrate on my lessons. I withdrew from my friends, who found me 'odd'. I still managed to hang on, though too many days off meant my school work was affected.

Strangely enough, the adults around me never suggested I saw a doctor. In those days one was just considered to be a 'difficult' adolescent. In any case, the suggestion of a consultation with a doctor would have filled me with horror. I had to cover up my real problem.

Boarding school, my parents decided, and I went along with this idea. A new start, a different atmosphere. I had read so many books about girls' boarding schools and I knew it was all going to be jolly good fun . . . new friends, midnight feasts and lots of practical jokes. Above all there would be no travelling to and from school. The daily journey to my present school was becoming a nightmare in itself. Being privately coached soon helped me to regain my educational level and my confidence was returning when I passed the entrance exam to the new school.

It took a term for the novelty to wear off. The feelings of

anxiety which had been pushed below the surface began to trouble me once more and I felt increasingly trapped. Sleeping in a dormitory with rigid rules about not talking after lights out and no reading in bed left me with too much time alone with my thoughts and my out-of-control imagination. Mealtimes meant more rules and there were no acceptable excuses to leave the table. Eating became a problem with so many people watching and noticing my jittery behaviour.

At first I was able to cope with services in the school chapel (two each day and three on Sundays) but, inevitably, as the panicky feelings began to recur I found it more and more difficult to sit still until the end of a service.

Lessons were becoming an ordeal too. I would watch the clock: twenty minutes until the bell goes . . . ten minutes . . . five minutes. Little wonder that I started to slip behind with my school work again when sitting through a forty-minute lesson was purgatory. The feeling of being trapped built up even when I was sitting near a door. There was, of course, no chance of asking to be excused; you might get away with it on one occasion if you could plead an emergency – but not a second time.

The last straw came when I was told that I had to propose a vote of thanks to a visiting lecturer. It meant standing up in front of the whole school to speak and I knew I couldn't do it. For days – and worse, for nights – beforehand, I lived with this terror, visualising how I was going to make a fool of myself, forgetting what I had to say, breaking down in front of the whole school. My imagination was as usual running out of control and I knew I would not be able to walk on to the stage, smile sweetly and say my piece.

On the day itself I was sick several times and the terror built up and up. There was no way I could tell anyone that I couldn't go through with it, and as the time approached I felt even worse. I ran away from school.

I went back, of course, and I won't go into details of my punishment and disgrace. This was fifty years ago, and no one then would have considered that I might actually have needed help for a psychological problem.

I asked my parents to take me away and let me return to the local high school. Panic attacks and daily assembly would be preferable to a twenty-four-hour school environment. I said I was unhappy at boarding school and told some lurid stories about life in that eminently respectable establishment. Being unhappy was reason enough where my sensible parents were concerned, but I was grilled by the headmistress, house mistress and other members of the staff who insisted on being told why I wanted to leave their precious school.

Was I leaving because I was unpopular? I was indignant about that as I had many friends. Anything wrong at home? Death in the family? Bankruptcy? Divorce? I looked at them blankly and then explained that I was suffering from delayed shellshock after my – mostly imaginary – experiences during the Blitz. Did they believe me? I never found out.

It was such a relief to make yet another fresh start that I felt practically normal again. It didn't last, of course, but as the old feelings crept back, the time had come to do something about the problem. Hauled up before the head, I found out that at the age of sixteen I could at last explain *why* I was invariably late for school.

At last the adults were sympathetic. During assembly I was allowed to slip into one of the side rooms if I felt unwell. Better still, I was not forced to attend assembly at all but could wait in the classroom until the other girls returned. My form teacher let me sit near the door and I had permission to slip outside the class for a few moments if the tension became unbearable. Would you believe it, as soon as I ceased to feel under pressure I found many of the hitherto impossible situations I had avoided before became tolerable; now I could talk about the things that bothered me and tackle problems such as standing on my head in PE or hanging upside down on the wall bars in the gym, both of which activities invariably made me feel sick and dizzy.

I would take a packed lunch instead of eating with the crowd; but that didn't last long, as I found I was missing out on most of the news and gossip, so I was soon back lunching with my friends. The best thing was that nobody thought there was anything peculiar about me.

But there was one problem I felt unable to face. I had happily sailed through my music exams and the day came when I was told that I had to play the piano at assembly. To play in front of the whole school, knowing that many girls would be only too eager to criticise my performance, was unbearable.

Again the nights of frantic anticipation. I could imagine all the things that could go wrong. I could see all the gleeful faces as the whole school enjoyed hearing me make a fool of myself.

Why did I not just refuse to play? I could not bring myself to do it. I couldn't run away this time, so I cracked my thumb joint with a hammer. A difficult 'accident' to explain at the hospital, but I ended up with my arm in a sling and an overwhelming feeling of relief at the honourable way of escaping from my ordeal. I now suffer from chronic arthritis in my hand as a reminder.

I scrambled through my exams. There were too many gaps in my education for me to do really well, but at last I reached my final day at school . . . and I didn't want to leave.

Even travelling was no longer a bugbear. I attended a

secretarial college, travelling into the centre of London every day. The fears were all behind me and I could look ahead to a future as a normal person. A relative in the Foreign Office got me a job in MI6. Sounds exciting, but it was basically just another secretarial post where I was very happy and made many good friends.

I was engaged to be married, although we had a five-year wait ahead of us as Michael had to get his law degree and qualify as a solicitor.

One winter's day I was just recovering from a bout of flu and waiting at a bus stop on my way to work. Disaster. Back swept the terrifying feelings that I thought had gone for good. I didn't know how to handle them and staggered into a shop, where I asked for a glass of water and telephoned for a cab to take me the ten miles home from the centre of London. Of course, as soon as I arrived home I felt perfectly all right apart from being a bit shaky. After-effects of the flu, I decided, and opted to take another week's sick leave to make sure I had completely recovered. I never dreamed that the old demon had raised its ugly head again.

I put the episode out of my mind and happily travelled back to London the following week. Back at the same bus stop, and my knees started to wobble and my breathing speeded up. It was all coming back. Luckily a bus came along and, jumping on to it, I broke the sequence of panic.

I couldn't believe I was back to square one, but I became increasingly worried abut my journey to work and organised my day around a variety of coping strategies. There was no way I could avoid the bus journey to the centre of London and, desperate for human contact, I would talk to anyone else standing at the bus stop. I always carried a newspaper to look at while I waited, and when the panicky feelings started to build up I would dart into the nearest telephone box. (How I would have welcomed a mobile phone.) I would telephone my mother, the only person who knew about my struggle. Having once suffered from agoraphobia in her youth she would talk me through the feelings and encourage me to keep going.

Every day was a continual fight against rising panic and feelings of unreality. Every morning I felt sick with apprehension but I was determined to hide my distress. I could not bear anyone to know about it and dreaded making a fool of myself in front of other people; I was determined not to draw attention to myself though I may have looked somewhat twitchy and uncomfortable to anyone who studied me carefully as I stood at the bus stop. I carried a card on which I had written my name, address, date and destination.

When the real world started to slide and my memory played tricks I would read this over and over again to reassure myself that I really existed.

I would deliberately arrive at my office half an hour before anyone else so that I had time to have a cup of tea, sit down and recover my equilibrium. I loved my job and dreaded the fact that I might have to give it up, despite the misery of getting to the office each day. Sometimes when I felt really bad I would think of looking for work nearer home, but I knew instinctively that once I gave in the phobia would follow me; then I would give up the local job and retreat into my home. I had to conquer the problem before it conquered me.

I was not tackling the phobia correctly, any expert would tell you today. Face the panic, experience it and go through it, they would say – but I was trying to avoid it at all costs. Every time I experienced a severe panic attack I would become more sensitised and likely to have another one. Avoiding the panics enabled me to operate on an even level and live a normal life, but I am sure I would probably have overcome it more quickly had I known the modern way of going about it.

I combed libraries and bookshops looking for information about agoraphobia (panic disorder wasn't known to the lay person in those days). There was very little written for the sufferer, and what I could find frightened me even more.

I consulted a psychiatrist (I picked his name out of a newspaper, hoping to find an expert in his field). 'You are probably quite a nice young woman,' he told me. 'But you are obsessed with your symptoms which are caused by an anxiety state, and you will just have to learn to overcome them.' I had hoped some sort of treatment might be available but was warned off by the great man, who felt that as I did not appear to have any underlying problems and was managing to cope, any treatment might result in aggravating the condition rather than curing it. This was in 1953.

No treatment, just keep going! At least I had acquired one comforting piece of information: agoraphobia would not kill me and it would not ruin my life unless I let it.

Recovery would take me five years. It was very gradual but I tried to adopt an optimistic approach to life. Every day I would find something to enjoy. It may have been a compliment – oh how vain I was! – it may just have been enjoying the music of the buskers on the way to work; I have always responded to any kind of music. One spring, Piccadilly Circus was filled with multicoloured bubbles inviting the public to the Ideal Home Exhibition.

I talked to people – anyone who looked as though they might be responsive – so I was never alone. These tactics would do nothing for my panic attacks but they made me feel more cheerful. I learned to smile at everyone and was gratified to find that about 80 per cent of the public would smile back. Life was definitely looking up.

I still had trouble travelling around London. My office had moved to the bottom of Whitehall and I had to cross Parliament Square every morning. Sometimes I couldn't do it and would have to take a taxi, making some feeble excuse such as that I was late for an important meeting.

It was at this time that my future in-laws invited me to join them and Michael on a summer holiday to Wales. I gritted my teeth on the long journey but would not have dreamed of admitting that I felt nervous. My father-in-law to be had been my family doctor all my life – but I never consulted him about my agoraphobia!

I felt relaxed and at ease with my second family, but then Michael announced that he and I were going to walk up Snowdon. Remember I couldn't walk across Parliament Square without feeling ill. I was really stuck. No way was I going to let on that I couldn't face that mountain.

It could have been worse. I kept my head down all the way as I found the open sky too vast and overpowering. I had blisters on my feet and took off my shoes as I felt happier concentrating on my sore feet than on any panicky feelings.

I have photographs to prove we reached the summit, but I couldn't wait to get to the bottom again, pleased to find I felt a sense of achievement. Two weeks later I was back in a taxi circling Parliament Square to get to my office in Whitehall.

Gradually it all faded. I hardly realised how much I was progressing until it became obvious that my nerves were no longer dominating my life. It takes some time to appreciate that one is really free. The biggest bonus was discovering that all the other anxieties disappeared, and instead of being a permanently anxious person with many devastating fears I discovered that I had become less fearful than most of the people I knew, that having trained myself not to worry, *I didn't worry*. It is possible to change one's life around.

I have described how my life changed when I had overcome my fears, but my crowning success was my wedding day. Four hundred guests in a London church in the middle of Piccadilly – one of my 'panic spots' some years earlier. The service was long and I thoroughly enjoyed every moment without even a frisson of fear. My self-confidence was so high I felt like floating off the ground. I will never forget that day.

6

A breath of fresh air

He's breathing in all the time when he should be breathing out and that puts him out all the way along. He can't get back into phase with it except by breathing in twice running.

N. F. Simpson, *Resounding Tinkle*

First aid for your panic attacks and all other anxiety problems: you must make sure you are breathing correctly. The main cause of so many of your frightening symptoms is that you are quite probably hyperventilating – overbreathing.

Holding our breath is a normal response when we are suddenly surprised or in some kind of danger – a response that is usually corrected automatically when the danger has passed as we gasp with relief and inhale, filling our lungs with air. But for the chronically anxious person this does not always happen; her nervous system has been conditioned to react to dangers that exist only in her mind, and her body responds by remaining constantly on the alert with muscles tense and breathing fast and shallow.

Frederick Perls, author of *Gestalt Therapy*, describes

anxiety as 'the experience of breathing difficulty during any blocked excitement'. The average person reacts to excitement by increasing the rate and volume of her breathing; the anxiety sufferer, on the other hand, attempts to control her emotions by interfering with her breathing, deliberately trying to appear calm and controlled and hiding her natural urge to pant and gasp as she takes shallow breaths and blocks off her oxygen supply. During a panic attack she may fold her arms or clasp her hands across her chest – literally trying to 'pull herself together' – as she struggles for control. She cannot breathe correctly, and she is not aware of what she is doing as she tenses all the wrong muscles in a desperate attempt to appear normal.

No gasp, sob or call for help will pass her lips if she can possibly help it. How dreadful it would be to expose your weakness and emotions, she thinks. A person without anxiety problems, without the same need to display a brave front in a dodgy situation, will allow herself to let out a yell of fright, and her breathing will quickly return to normal when the cause of her fear has disappeared.

Breathing is not just inhaling, it is the full cycle of inhaling and exhaling. Normally breathing out does not require any effort since it just means letting go and allowing the muscles that lift the ribs and lower the diaphragm to relax. When the lungs are emptied, fresh air can then enter, but the amount of fresh air which can be inhaled depends upon how much has been exhaled, so you will see that breathing out properly is just as important as breathing in.

Everyone knows that the body needs oxygen in order to stay alive, but the rate and depth of breathing controlled by the respiratory centre in the brain is affected not by a lack of oxygen but by the concentration of carbon dioxide in the blood. If we overbreathe and take in more air than our body needs, too much carbon dioxide is 'washed out' of the blood, resulting in tension around the chest and shoulder area and producing chest pains which are often an extra source of anxiety for victims, who begin to believe these may be signalling a heart attack. Further symptoms can include dizziness and feelings of unreality, sweating, palpitations and pins and needles in hands and feet.

Here's a letter to PAX from George (twenty-five):

I have so many phobias but it seems extraordinary to admit to a phobia of breathing. I suppose it is that I'm afraid if I can't catch my breath I might expire on the spot. The smallest thing that startles me or makes me jump and my breathing is all over the place. It's not just the huffing and puffing, it is all the other symptoms it causes. My heart speeds up, my hands feel numb, my chest is tight and painful and I know I am heading for a full-scale panic attack.

Many people who are chronic hyperventilators find that they may suddenly wake from sleep with night terrors. They assume that a bad dream has caused them to suffer a panic attack, but in fact it is the other way round. The sufferer's body is so used to overbreathing during the day that she continues to do so while she sleeps, causing her body to react by producing the familiar physical symptoms of fear which her subconscious mind translates into terrifying images.

Awaking suddenly, she naturally thinks that the nightmare has caused the acute feelings of anxiety. If breathing techniques are used to correct the problem during the day, it stands to reason that the body will eventually learn to breathe normally during sleep.

The emergency procedure to correct overbreathing, as I'm sure everyone knows, is to breathe in and out of a bag – a brown paper bag, we are told, but of course it doesn't have to be brown, or even paper. A plastic bag will do just as well – as long as you don't pull it over your head!

The object of the emergency exercise is that as you expel too much carbon dioxide you 'catch' it in the bag so that you can re-breathe it. This is a very successful technique, but some people get so attached to their paper bag that they become nervous of leaving home without it.

This is not a good idea. If you practise breathing correctly the paper bag will become obsolete. Remember too that you can use your hands in an emergency, cupping them over your mouth as you breathe gently in and out.

How do you know when you are breathing incorrectly and what can you do about it?

The kind of breathing associated with anxiety is in the upper chest. You can see this in the way the neckline moves up and down at each breath and the rate of breathing is fast. In contrast, slow breathing, using the lower part of the lungs with the emphasis on the outbreath, is a help in general relaxation and in relieving the symptoms of over-breathing.

Learning to breathe correctly is your first priority. Whatever kind of therapy you may be about to embark on, nothing will work satisfactorily until you have got your breathing under control

Concentrating on their breathing can sometimes become a problem as the anxious person, oversensitive to any change in physical sensations, may notice every little flutter and murmur of her heart and imagine that perhaps her pulse rate is speeding up and may run out of control.

Helen (forty): I find silence unnerving, which is why I like to have music playing in the background, particularly when I am trying to remain cool and calm and trying not to overbreathe, which is one of my main problems. I am no good at visualisation though I hope to improve with practice, but gentle music does make me calmer and more relaxed.

You are probably skimming over this chapter, but *stop*! You have got to make a real effort to follow the suggestions here. Reading about what to do won't help, though it may make you feel a bit happier to know that the symptoms you might be experiencing when you hyperventilate are not life-threatening.

There is a useful link between breathing and relaxation. Try this: tighten up all your muscles as hard as you can . . . very tight . . . then tighter. Then let go and relax. You probably found that as you tightened up you held your breath, and as you relaxed you let it go. This link between the outbreath and relaxation is a useful one and can be used whenever you practise.

You may also have noticed that your abdominal muscles contracted in the way they do whenever you are anxious or alert. This exercise therefore combines calm breathing with the relaxation of abdominal muscles.

Place one hand on the upper part of your chest and the other on top of your abdomen. Exhale first, then inhale comfortably. If you are doing this correctly your abdomen rises at the start of the breath, but if your chest moves first this is an inefficient kind of breathing.

Do it several times and try to breathe so that there is very little movement in the upper chest but plenty under your lower hand. Later on you will find that your back is also involved in breathing and your lower ribs spread sideways. Don't worry about this. Every time you breathe out do it *slowly* with a slight sigh, rather like a balloon gently deflating. After exhaling, pause a moment and let the breath come in just as much as the body wants; don't exaggerate the breathing in, let it happen. Combine the outbreath with relaxation whenever you practise

Two or three of these calm breaths are enough at the beginning of breathing practice. When you relax you will find that the body requires less oxygen; less carbon dioxide is produced so the breathing becomes shallow, slow and gentle.

Sometimes the anticipation of a future event can cause a build-up of anxiety which will inevitably result in changes in the breathing pattern. To be 'breathless with excitement' is a pleasant state for many people, but for the anxiety sufferer it just means that even the happiest occasion can be spoiled by agitated overbreathing caused by deliberately trying to block excitement.

If you feel that you can't catch your breath or breathe deeply, try this: Take a deep breath and hold it as long as you possibly can until you feel you are absolutely bursting. Don't cheat by taking little breaths. Time yourself; you will find that in about sixty seconds you simply can't keep from breathing any longer. Your body's reflexes will force you to take a deep breath.

Isaac Marks, *Living with Fear*

Singers and actors are taught how to breathe correctly in order to be able to project their voices and also to combat the thrill of the build-up before a performance, when incorrect breathing would cause anxiety which could escalate into acute and even disabling stage fright. Breathing correctly allows the excitement to be properly expressed; the performance then becomes enjoyable instead of being a dreadful ordeal.

Professor Marks describes how epidemics of mass hysteria with acute anxiety, overbreathing and faintness sometimes occur in groups of young women. I experienced this phenomenon myself when at the age of fourteen I was at boarding school. It was wartime in 1944 and we had a memorial service in the school chapel on the anniversary of Armistice Day. During a very emotional hymn, 'O Valiant Hearts', one of the girls threw a dramatic swoon and was quickly followed by another and another until the chapel was full of sobbing and fainting girls, who in a state of emotional excitement were all hyperventilating and passing out.

Me? Knowing that one of my 'funny turns' was coming on I had scuttled out of the chapel and was halfway across the playing field before the drama took place. The following Armistice Day, 'O Valiant Hearts' was banned and the choir sang 'O Lovely Peace' instead.

7

Medication

Gulp it down boy, it'll do you a power o'good.
Charles Dickens, Wackford Squeers
in *Nicholas Nickleby*

Edith is a typical anxiety sufferer. She is desperate to find the magic pill that will help her to overcome her panic attacks and agoraphobia but she has another problem – she has a phobia of drugs. Her GP has prescribed medication for her panic attacks but 'I can't take them because of the side-effects,' she says.

Edith has read the patient information leaflet enclosed with her made-up prescription listing an alarming number of possible side-effects that might be experienced and because, like the majority of anxiety sufferers, she always anticipates the worst, she immediately began to feel panicky, started to hyperventilate and blamed any unpleasant feelings on the drug itself, *even though she hadn't taken a single pill.*

Benzodiazepines

During the 1950s and 1960s, anxiety sufferers were constantly seeking a drug that would relieve their distressing symptoms. The benzodiazepines, of which Valium was the most popular, arrived on the scene and seemed to be the answer to their prayers. It became fashionable for women in particular to keep a bottle of these tranquillisers in the medicine cupboard to turn to in times of stress. Coping with children, marriage problems or an argument with a neighbour, all became reasons to swallow a pill with a cup of tea, knowing that although it would not remove the cause of her stress problem it would at least calm her nerves and help her to face the day. No wonder these magic pills became known as 'Mother's little helpers'.

Everyone, patients and doctors alike, began to regard benzodiazepines as the answer to any problem caused by anxiety, stress and emotional upheavals. These drugs were a real boon for the overworked GPs, who could rarely spare the time needed to counsel patients but who were thankful to prescribe indefinitely for those who wanted to take these pills.

The trouble was that instead of using these tranquillisers to help them over a crisis, nervous people began to regard them as a permanent crutch to help them to limp through life.

It was hardly surprising that problems began to arise when patients who had been on benzodiazepines over a long period found themselves dependent upon them, and once the beneficial effects wore off they were faced with having to cope with withdrawal symptoms as well as the original problem.

Can benzodiazepines *cause* panic attacks?

Yes, they can. Side-effects and withdrawal effects can both cause panic attacks. This is confusing and has caused a great deal of distress – the very drugs which are supposed to stop panic attacks can actually cause them in some cases. Withdrawal of the drug can also cause problems and therefore must be done slowly under supervision.

If benzodiazepines are taken regularly, increasingly large doses are required. The body becomes addicted to them and withdrawal effects are experienced when they are missed. The withdrawal symptoms can mimic the original anxiety symptoms the drug was prescribed for and are caused by overdependence on it.

Doctors do not claim that tranquillisers 'cure' anxiety. The idea is simply that if a person gets so anxious that they cannot cope with everyday life then the drugs will help them to calm down enough to learn to cope again. At some point it is hoped that the patient will stop needing the drugs, though it is more likely that in a false state of tranquillity she will avoid thinking about the problem and how she might go about tackling it.

Kate suffered from social phobia; she had a fear of meeting people, of eating in public, of travelling on public transport and of the need to dash to the nearest lavatory suddenly.

I found that I was quite euphoric when I first started to take tranquillisers. I thought they were going to solve all my problems and I told myself that when they took effect I would be able to get back into life once more. I did feel calmer and less desperate about the situation. Then I had a new doctor – a woman – who told me it was time for me to stop relying on the pills. Had I been on a bus lately, she asked. 'Been to the cinema? Any parties?' Had I in fact tried to face up to any of the things I was afraid of or was I still trying to avoid them?

She decided it was time I had some psychiatric help and referred me to the local hospital. I have started on a course of cognitive behavioural therapy. It's tough, but at least I feel I'm getting somewhere at last. I have almost given up the drugs.

Beta blockers

These drugs work by damping down the peripheral effects of anxiety – sweating, trembling, palpitations, etc. They are best used in short-term conditions of disabling anxiety such as examination nerves or stage fright rather than in the prolonged anxiety of panic disorder and phobic states.

Beta blockers are usually prescribed for high blood pressure and irregular heart action; however, they are also a good remedy for trembling hands, racing pulse and other expressions of anxiety. The main drawback of these drugs is that they do have some side-effects, including depression and loss of libido. Also they often cause extreme tiredness and lethargy.

Antidepressants

Antidepressants have been used in the treatment of anxiety over the years. The latest in this family of drugs are known as the Serotonin Re-uptake Inhibitors (SSRIs). Prozac (fluoxetine) is now used by millions of people all over the world. More recently, Seroxat (paroxetine) arrived on the scene, and PAX has received enthusiastic reports from many members who say their lives have been transformed by this drug.

As usual, sufferers expect immediate alleviation of their anxieties, but it takes about four to six weeks for Seroxat to show any effects and unfortunately some people are inclined to give up too quickly. There are side-effects sometimes, but those who have persevered are very enthusiastic about the drug's efficacy.

We are told that Seroxat is a non-addictive drug, and that however long patients are on it they will have few problems when they eventually decide to stop. Latest reports show that this may not be as easy as it sounds; the drug should be phased out gradually, usually two to six months after the anxiety symptoms have died down.

Herbal medicines

Here is a strange phenomenon. Many people who have a serious drug phobia and refuse to take prescribed drugs will quite willingly try over-the-counter medications and herbal drugs without giving a thought to side-effects. I know of many people who seem to be mixing everything under the impression that the greater variety of non-prescription medication they take, the quicker they will feel better.

Remember, though, that 'natural' doesn't mean risk-free. 'Every pharmocologically active substance has the potential for damage,' says Vincent Marks, Emeritus Professor of Biochemistry at the University of Surrey. 'As well as having beneficial effects it can also interact with other substances and cause side-effects.'

However, the good news is that serious side-effects are rare and the danger of overdosing is far lower than with conventional medicine.

Everyone should always consult their doctor or pharmacist before combining herbal remedies with over-the-counter or prescription drugs. It is clear that some herbs can influence the way conventional drugs are absorbed, metabolised or eliminated from the body. Experts have already raised the alarm about St John's wort, which may interfere with AIDS, HIV and anti-rejection drugs as well as interacting with anti-epileptic medication and oral contraceptives.

St John's wort is used to help mild depression and anxiety, so it is common for people who are taking antidepressants such as Prozac or Seroxat to try this herb as well. But beware – taking both remedies may cause increased anxiety or cancel out the beneficial effects of the prescription drug.

Researchers have warned that bright sunlight can harm the eyesight of those taking St John's wort. A substance in the herb called hypericin can cause a reaction that damages proteins in the lens of the eye, making the lens cloudy and causing cataracts. Those taking St John's wort should wear hats and wrap-around sunglasses out of doors where there is bright sunlight.

In Germany depressed patients are more likely to take St John's wort (also known as hypericum perforatum) than Prozac. This is seen as another Continental peculiarity like the French penchant for suppositories. In 1994, sixty-six million daily doses of hypericum were prescribed by German physicians, mainly for depression and panic attacks.

St John's wort is a small plant 20–100 cm high, with flowers of five yellow oblong petals which produce a dark red juice when rubbed between the fingers. It grows on dry soils, on heathland and at the edges of woods. It flowers around 24 June which is St John's Day, hence its name.

A PAX member once told me that she had a very old book

of herbal remedies. Could she try and brew up her own concoction of St John's wort?

Answer: You could . . . but don't even think about it!

Homeopathy

Homeopathy is a safe and gentle system of medicine, offering a unique approach to resolving phobias and anxiety states that is finely tuned to each individual and will suit them alone.

Homeopathy is based on the principle that a disease does not attack the body but rather is the body's method of curing itself of something which is wrong. Samuel Hahnemann, a German doctor in the early nineteenth century, believed that any substance which actually induces symptoms similar to those of a particular disease is probably stimulating the disease-fighting systems in the body and so is able to cure the condition. Hahnemann taught that the smaller the potency of the drug administered, the more easily it is absorbed into the sick body, which would reject a stronger dose. The substances from which the homeopathic drugs are obtained would in many cases be exceedingly poisonous if taken in anything but minute quantities. In the dilute form in which they are administered they are absolutely safe.

Homeopathy is 'whole person' medicine. During the initial consultation a homeopathic doctor will note down a detailed history, taking into account the patient's lifestyle, personality, temperament and even general likes and dislikes. The doctor will not concentrate on symptoms alone, because two patients with exactly similar symptoms may need to be treated very differently.

Homeopathic remedies are widely available and 'first aid' kits can be purchased in pharmacies. They are cheap and safe, but homeopaths feel that anyone wishing to experiment should learn something about the subject generally before doing so.

Bach flower remedies

> The remedies used are all prepared from the flowers of wild plants, bushes and trees and none of them is harmful or habit-forming. They are used, *not directly* for physical complaints, but for the sufferer's worry, apprehension, hopelessness, irritability etc. because these states of mind or moods not only hinder recovery of health and retard convalescence, but are generally accepted as primary causes of sickness and disease.
>
> BACH handbook

The flowers are preserved in pure brandy and may be taken internally (four drops in a small glass of water), or applied externally to the temples, wrists or lips. In an emergency a few drops may be placed directly on the tongue.

Remedies suitable for anxiety sufferers would include:

Aspen	For apprehension and foreboding. Fears of unknown origin.
Rock rose	Terror, extreme fear or panic.
White chestnut	Persistent unwanted thoughts. Preoccupation with some worry.
Larch	Despondency due to lack of self-confidence and expectation of failure.

In particular the Rescue Remedy, a blend of rock rose, clematis, impatiens, cherry plum and Star of Bethlehem flower is recommended in cases of panic.

The Bach flower remedies are available at pharmacies and health food stores. There are few anxiety sufferers who do not carry the Rescue Remedy with them at all times!

8

Relaxation is Nature's tranquilliser

The cure for this ill is not to sit still,
Or frowst with a book by the fire.
But to take a large hoe and a shovel also,
And dig till you gently perspire.
Rudyard Kipling,
How The Camel Got His Hump

Kipling's advice does not seem particularly appropriate in a chapter on relaxation, but sometimes when we are all keyed up and twitchy it is necessary to work off our excess nervous energy before we can benefit from any relaxation practice. The fact that nervous anxiety, unlike fear and normal vigilance, has no way of discharging itself means that the nervous person continually spends energy trying to control the 'fight or flight' syndrome which forms part of her anxiety. As a result she is liable to suffer from tension states which derive as much from the need to control anxiety as they do from actually experiencing it.

When you learn to relax you help your body to replace the flight response with messages to loosen tensed muscles. By releasing tension you help to signal to the mind that your situation is not dangerous, that there is no need to run away.

You may think that you are reasonably relaxed as you read this, but stop and consider what your body is doing. Your teeth are probably clenched tightly together; your tummy muscles are tensed; your shoulders are hunched and your knuckles are white from clenched fists. Do you bite your nails, fiddle with your hair, coil your legs around each other, frown and wrinkle your forehead? Anxiety and muscle tension go hand in hand; when you are alert and on guard, the muscles tense for action, and just as muscle tension is associated with arousal and anxiety so relaxation can induce feelings of calm.

Before a state of relaxation is possible it is important to get rid of some of the excess nervous energy that is making you feel so uncomfortable.

Exercise a dirty word? Many people who suffer from nervous disorders cannot tolerate the idea of exercise. To them the increase in the pulse rate as the body warms up and the inevitable huffing and puffing as they overbreathe are all indications of increasing anxiety, and the possibility of an approaching panic attack is so alarming to the oversensitised person that she will give up straight away.

Do not try to follow an exercise videotape at this early stage; you probably wouldn't last longer than two minutes. Think back to nursery school when you were told to touch your toes, swing your arms around pretending to be a windmill, hop from one foot to the other and stand on tiptoes trying to reach to the ceiling. All such simple acts, but they all mean that you are actually taking action and releasing tension.

When you feel ready to try some relaxation techniques, there's something I have to tell you: if you are going to benefit from these exercises you have to realise that, instead of constantly struggling for control over your anxiety and panicky feelings, you are going to relinquish this control.

This may sound alarming and I warn you that if you are not prepared for it you may well begin to feel the dreaded sensations of fear creeping over you. If you have a therapist guiding you through this stage, they will reassure you that you are not really losing control – your body is so unused to feeling relaxed that it sends out alarm signals to your wary mind, always on the alert to anything unusual.

It is important to work out your own relaxation techniques and to practise the exercises that you find most comfortable. Lying on a bed or on the floor in a silent darkened room may be soothing for some people, but those who are in a chronically nervous state may find such a setting oppressive and disturbing. Select the surroundings in which you feel most comfortable and at ease. If you find music soothing, have your favourite recording or radio station playing softly in the background. Settle yourself in a relaxed position – lying down or sitting in a comfortable chair. Remember, though, that you want to relax, not fall asleep.

Take a deep breath through your nose and release it through your mouth – allow your mouth to remain slightly open so that your jaw is not tensed up.

Do you begin to feel more at ease? Probably not. Most anxious people become tense at the very idea of relaxing because, as I warned you, any suggestion of 'letting go' means abandoning control. It is important to understand that you are about to lose control of your body by actually learning *how* to control it

Your first attempts at practising relaxation seriously may result in a heightened level of anxiety because you are not used to being without tension. You can alleviate this by demonstrating for yourself that your body, though relaxed, is still your own.

Open and blink your eyes, cough or move to another position. As you do so you will immediately find yourself back in the present, your level of anxiety will drop and you will be able to continue.

There are a number of methods of relaxation but all are variations of a basic technique. It is important when choosing a relaxation CD or cassette to ensure that the voice of the instructor does not grate on your nerves! So many people have made recordings, some of which are very good indeed (others just churn out the identical exercises that you can read in any book), but if you don't like the timbre of the voice or the accent, this will irritate and you won't be able to concentrate.

Recordings are usually about half an hour long and can get very boring. I would suggest that you don't try and listen to the whole thing in one go. You may progress to this at some future date, but for now take it one step at a time.

If you are not listening to a recording or are just working on what you have read, I would suggest that you start by concentrating on one part of your body and practise on this at first.

Hands would be a good starting point. Hands are not threatening; they are easy to control. Clench your left fist, and as you tighten up, concentrate on the tension in your hand, fist and arm. As you relax these muscles, note how loose they feel when you release the tension. Repeat this with your right hand and then with both hands together.

Shake your hands loosely as if you were flicking water from your fingers.

Relax with one hand cradled in the other. It is impossible to grip your hands tightly when they are cradled in this way, so always hold them like this when you are sitting down.

Head and face

Anxiety sufferers are particularly prone to tension in the head area; think of that 'tight band' round the forehead causing those headaches, blurred vision, buzzing in the ears, difficulty in swallowing, a 'lump' in the throat. There is even a clinical name for the latter – *globus hystericus* – a sinister name for a lump that is not really there!

Feel the muscles in the back of your neck by grabbing them in the way that you would pick up a kitten. If you are relaxed the muscles will be soft. Keep hold and slowly move your head forward so that it is tense, then let it relax again. Learning to recognise when your muscles are strained will help you to become more relaxed. Tensing up and relaxing your shoulder muscles a few times will also help.

Acupressure combines the power of massage with the pressure points used in acupuncture. To relieve a tension headache apply firm pressure with your thumb on the web between the thumb and forefinger of your other hand. Keep the pressure on for a couple of minutes, then release.

Sit comfortably and accept that you are in control of all the muscles you are moving. Wrinkle up your face, raise and lower your eyebrows and screw up your nose. Frown as hard as you can and then let go, relishing the feeling of relief. Push your tongue hard against the roof of your mouth, screw up your eyes and then let go again. Go through this routine two or three times until you really appreciate the relief from tension each time you relax the muscles.

Neck

Turn your head to look first one way and then the other, keeping your shoulders straight.

Bend your head from side to side, keeping your shoulders level.

Roll your head round, then drop it forward and lift it, keeping your shoulders down.

Chest and shoulders

Circle your shoulders to relieve muscle tension and improve circulation.

Pull your shoulders upwards and shrug several times. Bend your elbows and tense the muscles of your arms, then relax as you straighten them. Tilt your head backwards. Arch your back upwards and forward, then hunch yourself up pulling your shoulders forward. Release and shake your upper body gently.

Tummy and bottom

Pull in your stomach as hard as possible then 'push' it outwards. Imagine someone is going to punch you in the middle. Tighten up your buttocks and clench them together. Release.

Legs

Stiffen your legs and straighten your knees. Clench the muscles of your calves, press your heels down and stiffen your feet, pointing them upwards. Release.

Ankles, feet and toes

Curl up your toes and press your feet down. (If you get cramp easily in your feet, only do this for three seconds at a time.) Hold for a few seconds and relax.

If you want to listen to a recording on progressive relaxation there are several extremely helpful ones obtainable from the self-help organisations – see the end of this book.

Relaxation is not going to cure your anxiety or panic attacks but it will help you to bring down your general level of anxiety to a manageable degree.

In between your periods of relaxation practice, remember to work off some of that nervous energy referred to at the beginning of the chapter. Try to take some sort of physical exercise each day, though if you have not exerted yourself for some time be careful – don't be too energetic at first, and don't frighten yourself when your body warms up and your heart beats faster than usual.

And remember – there is nothing like a good laugh to fill the lungs with oxygen and banish tension!

9

Dizziness

He that is giddy thinks the world turns round.
William Shakespeare, *Love's Labour's Lost*

Could Shakespeare have had some experience of dizziness, like other famous victims of this debilitating disorder such as Julius Caesar, Martin Luther and Jonathan Swift?

Dizziness is the second most common complaint people bring to doctors. Forty-two per cent of adults report vertigo or dizziness to their physicians at some time in their lives. Eighty-five per cent of dizziness is caused by dysfunction of the inner ear. Dizziness is scary, it causes people to feel they are out of control.

Dr Jeffrey Kramer,
The Dizziness and Balance Center, Illinois

'I suffer from frightening dizzy spells,' wrote a PAX member. 'I am worried I may have some problem such as a brain tumour but I have had tests and my GP says it is all in my mind.'

Many of the people who write to PAX complain of dizziness and say it is one of the reasons they have become afraid to go out.

Most of us have had brief dizzy spells at some time, but some unfortunate people have attacks that last for several hours. They recur frequently and cause nausea, sweating and such disorientation that the sufferer cannot stand.

In the past when patients described the symptoms doctors routinely blamed their emotional conflicts, but although stress can make symptoms worse, recent studies have found no basic emotional disorder in the majority of sufferers.

In the nineteenth century this condition was named 'Menière's Disease' after Prosper Menière, the French doctor who first described it scientifically.

A good test of whether dizziness might be caused by psychological conditions such as anxiety is for the sufferer to deliberately hyperventilate (breathe rapidly). If he experiences numbness or tingling in hands and legs it is probably the overbreathing that is causing the problem. However, if dizziness occurs with nausea and disorientation then it is more likely to be caused by a physical disorder and needs to be checked by a doctor.

Sufferers from low blood pressure who experience dizziness should also see their GP. Brief episodes lasting less than a minute or two in older people are most likely to have a physical cause such as a disorder of the inner ear or arthritis in the neck.

Another common cause of dizziness is debris floating in the inner ear. This is called 'benign positional vertigo' (BPV), an alarming and disabling condition affecting twice as many women as men. Tiny crystals which have broken away from the parts of the ear that help us balance are the source of the debris. Key symptoms of BPV are violent dizzy spells that come on when lying down, turning over in bed, looking up or bending forward. These attacks cause a type of nausea that resembles seasickness. BPV can follow on from a viral infection or head injury.

Unfortunately many family doctors don't realise that there is an instant cure for BPV, and many sufferers are only prescribed motion sickness remedies. However, neurologists at the Medical Research Council's Human Movement and Balance Unit in London say that head exercise may cure the problem faster.

Dr Michael Gresty says that the exercises – called 'Epley's Manoeuvres' – will cure 7 per cent of cases after just one session and a further 20 per cent of cases after just two sessions. The exercises involve tilting the head at a certain angle and then rolling it backwards to the side. Some GPs will perform these manoeuvres; others will refer patients to a neurologist or ear specialist.

Vertigo

In the medical context, 'vertigo' is simply a technical label for the symptoms of perceptual disorientation which can be due to a wide variety of causes.

A perceptual cause for panic attacks and phobias?

An American psychiatrist recently suggested that 90 per cent of phobias are due to an easily diagnosable inner-ear dysfunction and not to emotional illness. He noted that most inner-ear-based phobias respond favourably to a series of anti-motion sickness and related medications, and that most panic episodes are related to a similar underlying physical disorder.

Dr Harold Levinson is a member of the American Medical and Psychiatric Association and is Clinical Associate Professor of Psychiatry at New York University Medical Center. In his book *Phobia Free*, Dr Levinson explains and diagnoses the physical components of phobic behaviour, showing us that a fear of travelling, for example, may be the result of an inner-ear failure to handle motion input – resulting in a panic attack. A fear of getting lost or going far from home could be explained as a simple directional dysfunction within the inner-ear system. A fear of heights might result from a sense of imbalance.

An integral part of our anxiety-control network is located in the cerebellar-vestibular system – the inner-ear system. If this system is weakened the entire anxiety-control network may be affected and the body may not be able to regulate anxiety, so that even a moderate amount of anxiety can escalate into acute fear and panic.

One of the functions of the inner-ear system is to act as a gyroscope controlling balance. If this balance system is impaired it can be further unsettled by heights, lifts, open spaces and many other situations. When you are unbalanced and dizzy you experience anxiety. Sense of direction can also be affected; you can become hypersensitive to motion which may cause different kinds of travel phobia. Bright, flickering lights, even certain colours or patterns can trigger anxiety, as the inner-ear processes all visual information. In the same way, because all sound information is filtered, sequenced and tuned by the inner-ear system, impairment may cause hypersensitivity to loud and piercing noises.

Causes of inner-ear dysfunction can be severe or repeated ear or sinus infections, glandular fever, concussion or a number of other disorders. Also, fluctuating hormone levels, often due to pregnancy, menstruation or the menopause, may be a cause. As many people have discovered, drugs or withdrawal from drugs can also cause acute anxiety and phobias, particularly agoraphobia which may also be due to inner-ear dysfunction.

Medications which specifically target the inner-ear system include a variety of anti-motion sickness drugs, antihistamines, vitamins and stimulants known to improve vestibular functioning. These medications often result in rapid and dramatic improvements in phobic behaviour and related anxiety problems.

Medication may well improve any problems in the inner-ear system, but remember that the psychologically triggered anticipatory anxiety may well remain and will have to be treated by other methods, such as cognitive behavioural therapy and graduated exposure to the phobic situations or objects that are causing distress.

When I wrote about Dr Levinson's book in the PAX newsletter, I received one of the biggest reactions ever from members who felt that many of their balance and dizzy problems led to acute anxiety and panic attacks because they had no idea what was happening to them.

Understand what is causing strange feelings and the fear will go

Sally: A few weeks ago I was walking round the supermarket. It has been months since agoraphobia restricted my life and I now have no fears of shops, public places, open spaces or anything at all.

Suddenly I was aware that everything had become blurred and I felt unsteady. Heavens! Memories of the old problem came flooding back . . . but the fear was not there, only this feeling of being off-balance. I knew that during my phobic years the fear would have been rising, I would be looking round for a way of escape and wondering *what if* . . . I faint, have a heart attack, throw up, etc. Of course I was concerned, because I was feeling dizzy and couldn't see properly. Suddenly I realised what had happened – one of the lenses had fallen out of my glasses! Knowing what had caused the feelings of unsteadiness and knowing there was a logical reason for them meant I had no reason to fear them.

Another PAX member:

Could natural remedies help my vertigo? After a bad cold I had a severe and frightening attack. I couldn't lift my head from the pillow and the room was spinning around. My doctor said I had labyrinthitis and prescribed pills for the dizziness. They helped a little but the doctor said there was nothing else he could do and it would gradually wear off after a few days, which it did. I am nervous that this might happen again; are there any natural remedies?

I once wrote in the newsletter about the time when I had labyrinthitis. It is very unnerving, and apart from the appalling sensations when the whole world seems to be spinning round it is always accompanied by acute nausea.

The labyrinth is the balance organ in the inner ear. It is vulnerable to viruses, which are a common cause of vertigo. Attacks of labyrinthitis do ease in time, but can in some cases last for several weeks.

Obviously the patient's GP will prescribe drugs to help the

condition, but a number of people writing to PAX suggested some home remedies they felt were helpful.

A warning – large doses of aspirin and excessive alcohol could make the problem worse and the patient should cut out salt, strong coffee and nicotine.

Drinking two glasses of pineapple juice each day and taking gingko biloba may speed up recovery. Patients wanting to try gingko biloba should first check with their GP if already taking prescription drugs.

A hot drink before bed will clear the nasal passages. A quarter teaspoon of cayenne pepper in hot water with two teaspoons of honey (10 ml) and the juice of a lemon was my grandmother's guaranteed cure.

Low blood sugar levels are often thought to be a common cause of dizziness, and naturopaths advise patients to look carefully at their diets. Foods should be eaten in as near to their natural state as possible. Cut out fatty foods and processed foods such as white sugar and eat plenty of fresh fruit, vegetables, whole grains, pulses, lean meat and fish, and make sure you eat regularly.

Aromatherapy

Those who suffer from low blood pressure who also experience dizzy spells should see their GP. However, if the dizziness is due to a temporary fall in pressure then the symptoms may well respond to aromatherapy. Use invigorating oils such as black pepper and rosemary, and for a stimulating bath add three drops of each essential oil to the water.

Acupressure

In straightforward cases of dizziness try using a pressure point in the foot. It is between the big toe and the second toe, about two inches down from the tips of the toenails. Press the point firmly with your thumb and massage with small circular movements for between one and three minutes about six times a day.

Chiropractic

If you are suffering from neck problems as well as bouts of dizziness, a chiropractor may be able to help as attacks could be caused by misalignment of upper neck joints. These joints contain nerves that control the balance of the head and ensure that the eyes are level. If the joints are not aligned correctly then nerve signals may cause dizziness. Chiropractors can manipulate the upper neck and the area lower down the spine to correct this.

Phobia sufferers often feel dizzy in supermarkets or shopping centres because they are unable to ignore irrelevant movements going on around them. Disturbed by too much action and too many people moving in their field of vision and becoming overwhelmed by a barrage of stimuli, they feel they are going to fall over or faint. Most sufferers will describe these sensations, and we begin to understand why 'fear of the market place' is not such a bad description of the more severe problem of agoraphobia. Sufferers who prefer to go out after dark or who feel 'safer' when wearing dark glasses are subconsciously trying to cut down on the disturbing stimulus of sound and noise that is going on around them.

'When I get dizzy my eyes play tricks and I can't breathe normally. I really feel I am going to die . . .'

To the chronic anxiety sufferer, desperate to gain control over the physical manifestations of the condition, this is where she must start . . . learning to breathe correctly is the first step to recovery.

10

Phobias

I will show you fear in a handful of dust.
T. S. Eliot

'If phobias were as common as names for phobias they would outnumber common colds,' says Donald Goodwin (*Phobia, the Facts*). The reason for so many names is that people can become phobic about almost any object or situation. Classifying phobias by the feared object or situation – a common practice in the nineteenth century – can be performed by anyone with a little Greek or Latin.

Professor Goodwin goes on to say:

One reason for so many names for phobias is that doctors have long recognised that fancy names for phobias are comforting and even therapeutic. The psychiatrist E. Fuller Torrey compared psychiatrists with witch doctors. 'Both,' he said, 'make you feel better because of the certainty exuded by the "authority figure", the diploma on the wall, or the proper headdress, bones and rattles, and finally because the authority in each case gave the condition a name.'

It is impossible to count the number of phobias that exist because they are limitless. There is an American website that lists (at the time of writing) some 600 phobias. By the time this book is published this number will probably have doubled.

Trying to count and name phobias seems a pretty pointless exercise. I receive letters from people saying that they are suffering from such and such a phobia that I have never heard of and I then have to ask them to explain what it is that they are frightened of.

A leaflet issued by the Royal College of Psychiatrists states:

A person with a phobia has intense symptoms of anxiety . . . but they only arise from time to time in the particular situations that frighten them. At other times they don't feel anxious. If you have a phobia of dogs, you will feel OK if there are no dogs around. If you are scared of heights you feel OK at ground level, and if you can't face social situations you feel calm when there are no people around.

This is not a true picture. A phobia is a fear which is severe enough to affect someone's whole life; a fear that is irrational, excessive and which the sufferer feels is uncontrollable. You might believe from the paragraph above that the phobic person becomes anxious only when exposed to the object of his fear or the situation where he feels distressed, but a true phobia affects the sufferer *all the time*, as his mind is continually concerned with the problem. He lives with it all day and every day and often can think of little else.

This is what distinguishes a phobia from the everyday fears

most people experience. You can be terrified of a snake if you see one, but in this country it is an unlikely occurrence unless you go to a zoo. The person with a snake phobia will worry about snakes every day of his life, will avoid looking at a book in which there might be a picture of a snake, will never watch wildlife programmes on the television. He will dream about snakes and allow his imagination to run riot, conjuring up thoughts and images of the dreaded creature until he feels that the phobia is dominating his life.

Many of those with a snake phobia have never seen a snake, but it is believed that the human race has an innate fear of them. Many animals also have this fear – monkeys brought up in captivity without ever seeing a snake will still act fearfully when shown one. This example shows how such a dormant fear can be brought to life:

Penny (twenty-two): I'm not sure when my phobia started but I have a picture in my mind which I must have seen in a book when I was a child, of a snake dislocating its lower jaw in order to swallow a small animal which was disappearing down its throat. I have never seen anything so evil in my life though I try to tell myself it is just one of God's creatures behaving normally. But those vicious fangs and those baleful glittering eyes! The picture remains in my mind today. I avoid looking at books which might contain pictures of snakes, I never watch wildlife programmes on television and I would certainly never go near the reptile house at a zoo.

If you are prepared to try to overcome a snake phobia yourself – that is, your horror of books, pictures, any mention of the creature – there is one important point to remember. If you live in Britain it is 98 per cent certain that you will never see a snake in the wild. That being so, you do not have to touch one or even face one when you are tackling your fear. Not in real life, that is. The fear you have to overcome is in your own imagination. That is what you have to get under control.

Isaac Marks, leader of the behaviourist school of psychology in this country, says:

> Behavioural treatment does not assume that phobias are symbolic transformations of hidden difficulties ... instead it regards the phobia or obsession itself as the main handicap and tries to eliminate it directly not by trying to uncover unconscious meanings but by teaching the sufferer how to face those situations which trigger his discomfort so that he can eventually come to tolerate them ... Effective behavioural techniques known under various names have in common the principle of exposure to that which frightens you, until you get used to it.
>
> *Fears and Phobias*

Once a phobia is established and *if no action is taken to control it*, the sufferer may be stuck with it for life. It won't go away on its own.

Often the phobic person will avoid seeking help because he is afraid of having to confront his phobic object ... but this doesn't happen straight away, it is a very gradual procedure. Before he even gets to this stage he must *think* about the object of his fear – in this case the snake.

'I can't bear to think about it,' people tell me, but this is avoiding the problem from the word go. You must visualise the dreaded creature in a harmless situation – say, coiled up asleep under a tree in an idyllic spot. All right, so you hate that picture, but if you can face it several times a day in your mind you *will* gradually learn to tolerate it.

If you are planning to take a holiday in the Amazon rainforest I would suggest that you seek help from a behavioural psychologist a few months prior to leaving this country.

The person suffering from simple phobia – an isolated fear of a single object or animal, for instance – is rarely seen by a psychiatrist. Often he does not realise that treatment is available, or he is so embarrassed by his problem that he prefers to suffer in silence.

More creatures great and small

Spiders (arachnophobia if you must)

Spiders – the creatures that appear to cause more alarm than any other, even snakes. 'I don't want to have therapy,' whimpered a young woman on the Esther Rantzen TV show. 'I just couldn't face a spider, let alone touch it. I don't want to even think about it . . .' This is a clue to the first step to recovery, as the snake phobic discovered. Think about the object of your fear. Professional help is available but the NHS waiting lists are long. Some of the phobia organisations and self-help groups have their own recovery programmes, and in the meantime there is much you can do to help yourself.

Before you confront your spider problem you must make sure you are in the right frame of mind. Practise your breathing, do your relaxation exercises. Remember that over-breathing upsets the chemical balance in your system and in itself this will cause increased anxiety. When you are ready . . . Don't try and go too quickly – but don't sit and think about it for too long or you might go off the whole idea.

Now try and concentrate on a positive approach, so before

you go any further spend a few minutes just thinking about the creature.

Make a list of nice things you can think of about spiders. Tell yourself that a spider's web is a beautiful and intricate piece of engineering and that a spider has as much right to its share of the planet as you have. There are no dangerous spiders in this country and any spider is much more frightened of you than you should be of it.

Can't bear to look at a picture of the spider? A PAX member wrote to say she had devised her own way of tackling the problem.

Fran (thirty-two): I drew my own spider! That is to say, I sketched a circle and labelled it 'spider'. I looked at it, touched it and laughed at myself. Just a round blank circle. Then I gave it two eyes and very gradually added six legs before realising, of course, that a spider has eight legs! That shows how little I knew about spiders. This may sound as if I am being flippant, but believe me this project was deadly serious.

So there I was, faced with a very realistic spider. I didn't like its face so I altered its eyes and gave it a smile. I stopped short of adding Miss Muffet and all her accoutrements and applied myself to my therapy.

It was *my* spider and I could control and erase it when I had had enough. I decided to look at a photograph of a real spider – something I had always avoided doing. I never watched natural history programmes on the television and if I came across a picture of the beast in a book I would turn the page quickly.

I select a photograph of a spider (that's the eighth time I've written down that word). It sits in the centre of its web. The web makes a pretty picture with the morning dew shimmering on the intricate piece of engineering that the spider has constructed. I can admire the web but I don't admire the hideous creature that sits in the middle of it, its evil eyes glaring balefully at me. I continue to look at the photograph and after a while touch the spider with the tip of my finger. Ugh!

But I felt that I had made a start. I continued to touch this picture and after a while could touch the spider without wincing.

I am making progress. I don't like it but realise that this is the way forward. Already I am not so obsessed, imagining spiders hiding everywhere, ready to jump out at me.

I have taken part in several television programmes where spider phobics have been promised that they can be cured of their phobia after spending half an hour with a psychologist/behaviour therapist/hypnotherapist. After this time the subject would be introduced to a red-kneed tarantula. (It's always a red-kneed tarantula.) It sits immobile on the table looking as though it wouldn't hurt a fly. To me it looks more like a furry eight-legged kitten. The phobic woman touches it gingerly with the tip of her finger.

Round of applause from the audience . . . but I know this isn't going to last. It just doesn't happen that way. People expect the problem will disappear suddenly, but in fact it takes time and a lot of hard work on the sufferer's part as they learn to face their fear, overcome their revulsion and control the physical sensations that hitherto have threatened to be overwhelming.

But back to the tarantula. It is not the immobile furry creature that is so alarming. I would have been more impressed if a bucket of ordinary house spiders had been tipped on to the table. They would have scurried in all directions and it is not just the phobic person who would have recoiled in horror, but a large number of the onlookers.

Small creatures and insects

Many of these move quickly and suddenly, often causing the oversensitised person to jump, breathe erratically and then interpret these reactions as fear. They may then say, 'I was frightened by a mouse,' when they were really just startled by the sudden movement. From such a small incident can a phobia develop.

When my four children were young they had a variety of pets. My eldest son's ambition was to breed a lilac-coloured mouse and the colony lived in a garden shed. I liked the little creatures and was happy to pick them up by their tails and let them run up my arm and round my neck; but the sight of a little harvest mouse scuttling across the floor would still have me jumping out of my skin and yelling, because I was surprised by the unexpectedness and the sudden movement.

A mouse phobia can build up to be as upsetting as a spider phobia if allowed to get out of hand. Mice can be quite unpredictable, even when tame, so acclimatising and conditioning yourself not to receive a fright with every movement is the way towards overcoming your fear.

You might also try visiting your local pet shop and watching baby mice or hamsters in their cages. They are much less mobile under those circumstances.

Again, watch wildlife programmes on television or read up on your dreaded creature. Getting to know its habits and personality will make it easier to understand and therefore less frightening.

Birds, bats and butterflies

Jean: I cannot walk my dog in the local park as pigeons and other birds congregate there, encouraged by people who throw bread and birdseed to them. I feel as though they might swoop too near me and knock me in the face. I can't bear their screams and squawks and I hate their beady eyes, scaly claws and fluttering wings, and I can't bear feathers. I'm afraid they might get up my nose and suffocate me.

I am ashamed to admit it but I cannot go near the lake in the park because of the ducks and geese. Because, again, people feed them, they charge through the water, quacking hopefully and the geese follow them up the bank. They are so frightening.

That PAX member, Jean, unfortunately went downhill and became housebound because her bird phobia upset her so much. Luckily she was able to get professional help and overcame the phobia relatively quickly. The therapist concentrated first on feathers, which turned out to be Jean's main problem. She then progressed to ducks, which were relatively easy as they weren't likely to take off and fly around.

It is usually the sudden movement that startles the anxious person, who feels that they cannot control a bird.

Birdsong is a sound that most people enjoy, but I wrote in an earlier book about John, then aged twelve, whose mother bought him recordings of the cries of seagulls – a sound whose 'dreadful melancholy' made him cry uncontrollably. The recordings were the first step in changing his perception of birdsongs so that he learned to think of them as joyful sounds and respond to them with pleasure. This was done with the help of an experienced therapist.

A phobia of birds is often linked with feathers. Jean wrote that she was afraid of feathers getting up her nose and suffocating her. 'They fly in all directions' and 'they seem somehow unreal' are some of the complaints of feather phobics. Feathers are in pillows and cushions and have a habit of working themselves out of the coverings. 'Butchers' shops at Christmas are horrific for me,' wrote a PAX member. 'I can eat turkey if I haven't seen it in its natural state, but I am having roast beef for my Christmas dinner.'

If your problem is birds, but includes a fear of feathers, tackle the feather fear first. Though you are repelled by the thought of touching one and though the sensation on your skin distresses you, you have to acclimatise yourself gradually.

One woman persisted in overcoming her fear of feathers by carrying around a tiny fluffy feather initially, gradually handling larger ones until she lost her fear of them.

Frogs

Snails and slugs cause feelings of revulsion in many people; the one thing in their favour is that they move very slowly. 'Slimy and disgusting – couldn't bear to touch them' is the general opinion. Frogs are also cold and slimy: they jump, and they live in gardens.

Megan came on a television programme with me some time ago. Her phobia of frogs meant that she wouldn't go into her garden at any time of year. It was unfortunate that her garden happened to be overrun by frogs. Poor Megan broke down in front of the TV cameras when she was interviewed. Her life was being ruined because of her frog phobia, she admitted.

On the programme with us was a well-known hypnotist. He could get rid of Megan's phobia, no problem, he told her. The TV station paid for Megan to have an expensive course of hypnotherapy and she was overjoyed at the thought of being freed from her fears.

Megan telephoned me some weeks later. The hypnotherapy hadn't worked, she said. Unfortunately, like so many people, she expected hypnosis to act like magic and cause the phobia to disappear.

Hypnosis has its uses, as I describe in another chapter, but unfortunately it is not magic, and the patient has to learn to relax and co-operate in the treatment as she gradually faces her fear and learns to overcome it. It won't go away on its own and hypnosis won't 'switch it off'.

Dogs and cats

How difficult it is to avoid these animals when almost every household in Britan owns a pet. Most of us dote on our pets and we find it difficult to understand those who cannot bear our friendly dogs and loveable cats.

But there are many people who are terrified of these animals and find it very difficult to avoid them. These days most dogs are on leads in busy streets but are allowed to run free in parks and open spaces, and although most are friendly there are others who aren't averse to nipping strangers or attacking well-behaved dogs, starting an unpleasant brawl.

Animal phobias almost always begin in childhood; if you do not have an animal phobia by the age of twelve you are unlikely to develop one in later life.

Donald Goodwin in *Phobias* says:

Boys and girls are equally likely to have animal phobias until puberty, after which girls are more likely to have them. These phobias do not run in families; little girls with cat phobias as a rule do not have parents with cat phobias. This has two implications: animal phobias are not directly influenced by heredity, and children do not learn them from their parents.

Sometimes animal phobias seem related to a specific event. A child gets bitten by a ferocious dog and thereafter avoids dogs, ferocious or otherwise. However, most animal phobias, like most phobias in general, seem unrelated to stressful events.

Even Sigmund Freud, one of the world's greatest explainers, had trouble explaining these phobias.

The child suddenly begins to fear a certain animal species and to protect itself against seeing or touching any individual of these species. There results the clinical picture of an animal phobia . . . Sometimes animals which are known to the child from picture books and fairy stories become objects of the senseless and inordinate anxiety which is manifest in these phobias. It is seldom possible to learn the manner in which such an unusual choice of anxiety has been brought about.

Dogs

Occasionally a dog phobia can be triggered by loud barking. Many anxiety-prone, oversensitive people overreact to sudden loud noises. They may well interpret this as a reaction to the dog itself and not just the sound of its barking.

Sometimes the phobia can be so extreme that the phobic

person refuses to leave the safety of her home in case she meets a dog. Dog owners are not very helpful in steering their dog away from people or keeping them on a short lead. ('If she hadn't screamed, Carl wouldn't have bitten her,' said my mother-in-law when her boxer attacked the next-door neighbour.)

The good news is that people with animal phobia probably respond best to types of behaviour therapy. Unfortunately the majority of those with animal phobias rarely consider seeking professional help . . . they just go through life avoiding the objects of their fears and putting up with a seriously restricted lifestyle.

Some people are so serously phobic it is impossible for them to overcome their phobia without professional help. However, if you feel your problem is mild enough – and you are brave enough – to do something about it yourself, here are a few tips.

As always, try to get your feelings of anxiety under control with the breathing and relaxing techniques discussed earlier.

First step – you *must* try to develop a more positive attitude towards your phobic object.

Write down the first thoughts that come into your head about dogs. They will probably look like this.

Dogs can be dangerous . . . they bite.

Dogs are smelly and their toilet habits are disgusting.

Dogs are noisy; they bark uncontrollably.

Dogs fight other dogs and kill cats.

Dogs attack children, causing terrible injuries.

Dogs spread diseases; they are generally a nuisance.

Just stop here for a moment and consider. These statements may sometimes be true but almost always it is the dog's owner who is at fault, not the dog itself.

Now *force* yourself to write down six positive things about dogs.

A dog is a faithful and loyal friend to its owner.

A dog protects the home against intruders.

A dog is children's loved companion.

Most dogs are friendly.

Working dogs are valuable to society.

Dogs don't have criminal tendencies – unlike an awful lot of human beings.

It is easy to say you should practise looking at pictures of dogs then touching the pictures, but a dog phobia can be as upsetting as a snake phobia and the revulsion of touching a photograph of a cuddly puppy can be just as distressing as touching the snake.

When at last you have progressed to the real thing, I don't have to warn you not to approach a strange dog without being 'introduced' by its owner; and don't stare into a dog's eyes as it will interpret this as an aggressive challenge. When you recover from a dog phobia you will realise what a rewarding relationship you can have with a dog.

I have quoted before the story of one woman's attempt to cure herself of her dog phobia. She summoned up the courage to buy a puppy, left it in her house while she went out shopping – and then was too afraid to go back into the house and face it.

Cats

Cats have a habit of making a beeline for people who feel fear or distaste. Animals like to please, and when they sense antipathy or dislike they try to right that with affection. This, in the eyes of the sufferer, can be perceived as an assault or a purposeful attempt by the animal to aggravate. Some people may experience a genuine physical reaction to a cat, as you can see from this case:

> I don't have to see a cat to know that one is in the room. Apart from a deadly fear of the creatures my body reacts physically and I feel nauseated, a rash erupts on the back of my hands and my breathing is affected. Above all, when I come face to face with a cat it is the eyes that terrify me. They have an unblinking stare that bores into you as if the animal knows what you are thinking.

It is possible that this sufferer's physical reaction is a genuine allergy to the animal. When she hyperventilates and breaks out in a rash she may blame this on the intensity of her fear rather than on a chemical reaction. By treating this medically, one aspect of the reaction to cats will be removed, making it easier to tackle the psychological symptoms.

One is tempted to say, 'When you are ready to tackle your phobia . . .' but you never will be ready while you are sitting around waiting for the signal. *Do it now.*

11

Miscellaneous
Strange phobias and true stories

*Arachibutyrophobia: A phobia of peanut butter sticking
to the roof of the mouth.*

I dislike all the weird and wonderful names for phobias and
this one takes the biscuit. It appears on the American website
which lists around 600 phobias.

Recently I had a telephone call from a medical student
whose friends had bet her £50 that she couldn't identify a
certain phobia. She couldn't find it in any medical books, she
said. It took me the whole afternoon to identify it and she
won her bet. Needless to say, it was a made-up phobia and too
rude for me to print here!

Here are a few unusual phobias I have come across in the
thirty-five years I have been involved in running *The Open
Door* and PAX.

Buttons	Leaves
Cotton wool	Navels

False teeth

Roses

Number 13

Colour purple

People with facial
disfigurements

Knives and scissors

Tissue paper

The sound of trumpets and
other brass instruments

Skeletons and human
bones

Amputees

A young woman who loved children, but had a fear of buttons, got a job in a day nursery where she spent a good part of each day buttoning and unbuttoning the children into their garments. She hated it at first but gritted her teeth and gradually overcame her fear.

This is known as counterphobic behaviour. Isaac Marks states:

> This is the attraction some patients have to their phobic situation or object so they seek it out repeatedly.
>
> Counterphobic behaviour may thus help the patient to overcome his fear by gradually familiarising himself with the phobia until it loses its frightening aspect.

In my first book I wrote about a man with a phobia of large leaves. He had to drive to his office each day down country lanes and had to plan his journey so that he could avoid trees and dense foliage by the side of the road. Summertime was very difficult for him but he had a very positive, even light-hearted attitude to the problem. 'My next-door neighbour is very anti-social, he insists on growing rhubarb against our party fence,' he told me. He made a good recovery after having private treatment, having felt he couldn't admit to such a phobia in an NHS hospital.

Other PAX members who eventually recovered from their

phobias were the two women whose problems were very similar in some ways. Angela, having found out the weight of a human head, became obsessed with the idea that her neck wasn't strong enough to support her head and had to wear a brace. Gillian believed that her head was so light that it would fly away. She did not feel safe unless her head was anchored by a scarf at all times.

Both women received intensive psychotherapy, eventually managing to shed their strange obsessions.

On the Esther Rantzen show a middle-aged woman was interviewed about her phobia of being kissed on the lips. There were some pretty ribald remarks from the psychologist sitting next to me in the audience. There was no way she could be treated, she insisted, as she would faint any time a man went to kiss her passionately.

It was unfortunate that Esther Rantzen and the audience were so fascinated by the woman's stories of the problems her phobia caused her that there was no time for the other phobic sufferers who were waiting to take part in the programme.

12

Body and soul

I'm more than a little sick...
Rudyard Kipling

Many people live in constant terror of being ill, and particularly of developing some terminal disease. They are not helped by the fact that much of the advertising for cancer research and other potentially life-threatening illnesses has relied heavily on presenting a dark and gloomy picture, resulting in the oversensitive souls among us becoming convinced that they are particularly susceptible to such illnesses.

We are well instructed by the media about what we should and should not do to keep healthy, and we are left in little doubt about some of the awful things that can go wrong if we smoke, eat the wrong things, get too fat or too thin or exercise too little or too much. We are told to feel our bodies for lumps, undergo smear tests and X-rays, stay out of the sun and present ourselves for regular health checks, blood pressure, cholesterol and blood sugar level tests.

We read alarming accounts in every publication of new

and unnerving medical procedures and personal stories describing how someone has suffered and survived every physical and mental disorder under the sun – with detailed descriptions of symptoms.

People with illness phobias need to be distinguished from hypochondriacs who have many imagined symptoms and illnesses. Phobics focus on one particular illness, and any symptoms point in one direction only – to the disease they so dread.

Phobias

- There is dread and anticipation of contracting a specific illness.
- Apart from the symptoms of acute continuing anxiety, the person knows she is not ill.
- The phobic patient does not gain from the phobia, unlike the hypochondriac who expects sympathy and continual reassurance from those around her.
- Most will go out of their way to hide their fears and only when desperate will submit to a medical test, which will not convince them that the dreaded disease is not apparent.

Hypochondriasis

- There is constant worry about ill health generally.
- Anticipation does not play an important part but symptoms of any illness will cause the person to experience fear.
- They sometimes convince themselves that they are ill and seek sympathy and attention from others.
- They may even appear to enjoy the situation.

and a new disorder . . .

Cyberchondria

Doctors have discovered a new disorder – cyberchondria. It is the mistaken belief that you suffer from all the diseases featured on the Internet. Doctors complain that they are made to carry out tests for rare or non-existent conditions because hypochondriacs come armed with information from websites or memorise impressive sets of symptoms.

An anxious person with an over-active imagination is most likely to develop an illness phobia if she has had some contact with a particular disease. Perhaps a member of her family had cancer, perhaps an acquaintance has died after a heart attack. As her conviction that she is experiencing similar symptoms strengthens, the signals of stress become more evident – with racing pulse, overbreathing and aches and pains due to muscle tension.

Body dysmorphic disorder (dysmorphobia)

Diane (twenty-four): I can't bear my face or any part of my body and feel so ugly and ashamed. I also suffer from blushing which is ruining my life. If I won the lottery I would have myself changed however much surgery cost. But I am really stuck with this horrible person and I dread to think about the future.

From head to toe, every part of the body can hold fears for some people. A very serious problem now receiving publicity is body dysmorphobia, where the sufferer cannot bear some portion of their own anatomy and will go to any lengths to change their appearance by plastic surgery.

Body dismorphic disorder (BDD) is a condition where sufferers have an obsessive preoccupation with a perceived defect in their appearance. An Italian doctor named Morselli coined the term in 1886 from a Greek word meaning misshapen. While many people are concerned about their looks, a person with BDD is so preoccupied with their appearance that it can handicap their life.

Sufferers sometimes hide or change their appearance and become depressed and demoralised. They tend to be secretive and reluctant to seek professional help.

BDD sufferers may also suffer from social phobia, obsessive compulsive disorder, hypochondriasis (fear of suffering serious illness), repeated body examination and weight monitoring, and trichotillomania (the urge to pluck out hair or eyebrows).

Sufferers often develop BDD in adolescence, when most people are sensitive about how they look. Areas which cause most concern to sufferers are nose, hair, eyes, skin, chin and lips. People will often seek treatment from a cosmetic surgeon before finally accepting psychiatric help.

Treatment for BDD is SSRI antidepressant drugs and cognitive behaviour therapy based on a structured programme of self-help, teaching sufferers to change the way they think and act.

> If you can't change your physical appearance you must change from the inside and learn to love yourself.

Monophobia – fear of being alone

If an agoraphobia sufferer becomes housebound they may develop a fear of being alone. Partly this is separation anxiety, worrying where their partner is and whether they might have had an accident, run away from home or something equally disastrous. Supposing they never came home, what would the phobic person do, how would they cope? All sorts of frightening thoughts run through their minds, all convincing them that they will never see their loved ones again.

But you *can* manage without other people constantly by your side. You must learn to let them go. You may say, 'I can't stay in the house on my own,' but this negative attitude will only increase your fears. You must learn to face up to the problem in a different way. Tell yourself, 'I feel bad when I am on my own but this does not mean I can't do it if I try.'

Sometimes it is not just being left that is frightening; it is being alone with yourself.

Who am I? This is the question that many sufferers ask themselves. Much of the time they feel out of touch with the rest of the world. Do you feel like this? Do constant anxiety and panic attacks drag you down so that you feel unreal much of the time? Of course you are depressed, but you are quite likely to feel that way because of the possibility that nothing will ever change, that you will never feel better, that no one understands, and that you are all alone.

There is one person who can help. You. But perhaps you don't really know that person, because you are frightened of yourself. When did you last take a look at your reflection in a mirror? Scary, isn't it? The person looking back at you doesn't seem to be anyone you know.

Wendy (fifty-one): I practise studying myself in the looking glass every morning as Alice has suggested in the newsletters. It is quite true that this can be a scary experience and I hadn't realised just how much I had avoided doing this in the past. It always started the thoughts such as 'Who am I? What am I doing here?' and many other disturbing questions.

Now I am able to accept myself as I am and find myself more relaxed and able to enjoy life without constant questioning. I make myself smile at my reflection and greet me every morning. I do think in recent years an awful lot of damage has been done in encouraging everyone to try and analyse themselves.

Overcoming the fear of being alone

You must practise staying on your own, in a room apart from your family, initially for just five minutes. Then practise staying in the house when everyone goes out. Keep a notebook and write down the length of time you lasted, aiming to add another five minutes every few days.

Most families are supportive but, again, people are funny and sufferers often don't want their nearest and dearest to know just how bad they feel. A pity, because if your partner, parents or children don't understand or are not given the opportunity to be helpful you can sink into depression and despair.

What a blessing is the mobile phone. I would have considered it a life-saver if I had had one in my agoraphobic years. For the person afraid to be on their own it is so important that they are able to be in touch with their helper. Aim at spending a couple of hours on your own with a telephone to hand. Knowing you can summon help immediately is the first big step, and you will find that your SOS will not be needed after all.

Try to spend longer and longer home alone during the day, slowly extending the hours into the evening and then into the night.

I will mention here the recording I made called *Panic Attacks*. If someone is on their own, particularly at night, it can be upsetting knowing there is no one to listen to their fears. The recording is fifty minutes long; in it I talk the sufferer through a panic attack and go through the breathing and relaxation exercises, giving encouragement and talking as a friend. Details of the recording are at the end of the book.

Some of the other phobia organisations have emergency phone lines with comforting recorded messages.

If you are alone and distressed, try rocking yourself backwards and forwards. You will have seen film of distressed refugees, survivors from disaster and those suffering from emotional trauma. When there is nothing they can do they sit on the ground and rock. Through the ages babies have been rocked in cradles and a child is soothed by the rhythmic movements when lulled in its mother's arms.

Rocking helps to relax the body and drain away tensions. No one really knows just how this works, but it seems likely that the rhythmic motion helps to counteract urgent messages which are being sent from the muscles to the brain. Anxiety and tension tighten up muscles but the rocking motion loosens them again. So don't feel foolish when rocking, but understand that it does help to release a little of the pent-up nervous energy that is adding to your tension and fear.

Sphincter phobia or Where's the loo?

Over the years I have come across many many women who have become social phobics and housebound because of their fear of being 'caught out' when needing to find a lavatory urgently. Because this is always at the back of their minds it becomes a reality.

Frankie (thirty-seven): For years I was afraid to go out of the house or travel anywhere at all. I was not what one would call truly agoraphobic but if I contemplated going out anywhere I would immediately want to spend a penny. It never worried me in my own home as I knew I could get to the toilet, but I felt that as soon as I *thought* about it I would have to go.

My GP was fairly sympathetic and made sure I was checked for any physical problems but I was all clear. 'It's only in your mind,' he told me, and suggested various exercises which I tried out – mental and physical. I practised all the usual techniques which every woman learns when she has had a baby – pelvic floor exercises and 'tightening up'. I didn't suffer from stress incontinence when you leak when you cough or sneeze, but all this didn't help much.

I was always in the habit of going to the toilet very frequently whenever I thought about urinating, whether I really wanted to or not. I read about one of the rules the Royal Family has of taking every opportunity of using the toilet – just in case.

This is where I was going wrong. Instead of giving in to every slight urge I had to learn to control them. I planned a timetable, checking every half hour and then seeing how long I could put off visiting the toilet. I would tell myself, 'I don't *have* to go,' and found that I *didn't*.

Putting this into practice was more difficult outside and my GP suggested that the whole problem was more widespread and an excuse not to go out. I am persevering, however, and I do feel that if I am trying to do something constructive it will help me recover.

Emetophobia – fear of vomiting

This is a very common phobia and very restricting. Someone with this phobia will avoid travelling if this produces feelings of nausea and will eat only food which can be trusted not to upset the stomach. This makes life unadventurous but bearable. Surprisingly, the person who has a phobia of *someone else* vomiting has a greater problem in some ways, as there is no way they can control the situation. Children and pets are prone to throw up without warning, causing acute anguish to the sick-phobic sufferer who can be thrown into a state of panic if someone burps, chokes or has a coughing fit which might possibly lead to vomiting. See Chapter 19 for details of the Gut Reaction self-help group.

Seasonal Affective Disorder

In days gone by as the winter solstice approached and the days became shorter, early man believed the sun was dying. It must have been pretty scary as, although it happened every year, people must have thought that perhaps *this* year was going to be the one when the sun actually disappeared, never to return. This must have caused universal anxiety at the time and perhaps this worry has come down the ages to us, resulting in depression and gloom.

In the past, fires were lit to try and encourage the sun to return, which is why we celebrate with lights and feasting when the daylight hours gradually lengthen. This is why the early Christians decided to adopt the winter solstice as Christ's birthday.

In earlier times our ancestors went to bed when daylight ended. They had worked hard through summer and probably rested and ate more in the winter. Today we find the dark mornings and evenings depressing; we have a struggle to get up in the morning, eat too much, exercise less and are generally at our lowest ebb.

'Becoming less active has a knock-on depressive effect,' says Professor Stephen Palmer, a health psychologist and director of the Stress Management Centre in London. 'People see friends less frequently and go out less. They tend to switch on the TV instead. Living life through the small screen can make you feel low. A small minority suffer a full clinical depression in winter, while feeling fine the rest of the year.'

This is Seasonal Affective Disorder or 'SAD' and it can be seriously disabling with some sufferers requiring hospital treatment. Millions of others, while not seriously ill, feel gloomier than normal. According to Jon Simmonds, secretary of the charity SAD Association, they are suffering from the winter blues – a milder form of SAD.

Many PAX members seem to be susceptible to SAD and write in their dozens to the newsletters each autumn.

Phillida (forty-nine): At this time of the year I feel a real urge to hibernate. My agoraphobic symptoms are worse and all I want to do is draw the curtains and sit indoors watching television or listening to music. I don't want to look out of the window at the dark and dreary afternoons. This time of year is so depressing.

'No one knows how many people suffer from SAD,' Jon Simmonds says. Symptoms include lethargy, loss of libido and a craving for food – sugar especially. They also feel run down, are loath to get up in the mornings and are prone to infections.

Researchers believe that reduced levels of sunlight trigger a biochemical imbalance in the hypothalamus, the area of the brain that co-ordinates our hormonal and nervous systems. One theory is that this increases levels of melatonin, released by the pineal gland during darkness to help us sleep. Melatonin levels have been found to be higher in the mornings with SAD, which may explain why sufferers often want to go on sleeping.

How to be happy when you are 'SAD'

For those suffering from SAD, light therapy boxes, at least ten times the intensity of ordinary domestic lighting, are available from specialist retailers with prices starting at about £100. These light boxes mimic the effects of the sun's rays by emitting enough brightness to penetrate the eye and stimulate the affected part of the brain.

For the best results it is necessary to sit in front of a light box for a couple of hours a day. It is also possible to get special alarm clocks that light up your bedroom while you sleep. As a result, your body's internal clock speeds up and wakes you gradually, so you don't feel so tired during the day.

Get as much natural daylight as possible, especially around midday. Leave your bedroom curtains open at night or, if you are used to sleeping in the dark, draw the curtains back as soon as you wake each morning to let as much natural light as possible into your room.

Switch on more bright lights around the house – this may be enough to get rid of milder forms of depression though not enough to treat severe symptoms effectively.

Fresh air is a great antidepressant and a vigorous walk can raise the body's level of serotonin, the chemical that improves your mood.

Stick to healthy eating guidelines and try not to overeat – a problem for many SAD sufferers. Eat more wholefoods and fruit and include protein with every meal. Don't skip breakfast and do eat a snack at bedtime to help you sleep. If you have a craving for refined carbohydrates which can raise the levels of serotonin, remember that these can lead to sudden drops in blood sugar levels.

Anyone suffering from serious depression in winter should go to their GP; the non-sedative antidepressant drugs such as Prozac and Seroxat have been found effective for SAD, especially when combined with light therapy.

A recent trial of the herbal remedy St John's wort found that it helped sufferers as much as light therapy.

Sleep problems

Alice: I have always been terrified of going to sleep. Actually I think it is really that I am afraid of dying. As a child I never went to bed without worrying about whether I would wake up the next morning. 'Could death creep up and take over from sleep?' I asked my parents. After all, they had taught me to pray, 'If I should die before I wake, I pray the Lord my soul to take.'

'Don't be morbid,' they said and the subject was dropped. Unknowingly, it was their avoidance of the issue that made it all the more frightening. After all, if my parents couldn't discuss it, there must be some reason why it was unmentionable.

The PAX postbag has always received many letters from people suffering from sleep disorders. Some have a phobia of sleep, often linked with a fear of death; others are worried about their inability to sleep, longing to be able to have a night free from tossing and turning and fretting that lack of sleep might be damaging to their physical and mental health.

Some people wake refreshed after less than six hours' sleep and it would be wasteful to have more; others find that even ten hours is not sufficient. It seems that good short sleepers are more efficient in the way they sleep and can recharge their batteries in a shorter time than others. It is the quality of the sleep which counts rather than the quantity. Good sleepers have an adequate balance between dreaming sleep (called REM sleep because it is accompanied by rapid eye movements) and the deep non-REM sleep. Both kinds of sleep are necessary and serve different restorative functions.

Chronic sleeplessness can increase anxiety symptoms and interfere with health, relationships and the ability to function effectively. Because chronic sleep disorders may be due to either medication or medical problems it is best to discuss these problems with your GP. If your sleep is poor or interrupted or you wake early feeling tired, it is possible the problem may be depression.

If you suffer from long-term insomnia you will know that the more exhausted you are the more aroused you become, too alert to sleep. Many anxious people so dread going to bed that they put it off for hours – then they are in such a jittery state and so exhausted they haven't a hope of relaxing into easy sleep. The actual routine of composing themselves for bed, lying down and waiting for unconsciousness is unthinkable. They would prefer to sit up all night in a chair and cat-nap.

A number of people have panic attacks while asleep – often caused by chronic hyperventilation, as we have seen. This can cause a phobia of sleeping and the sufferer dreads the hours of darkness.

Self-help manuals advise against cat-napping during the day. The body must be trained to sleep during the night only, they say, and any sleepiness in the daytime must be overcome by going for a brisk walk, or finding some activity that will keep the mind busy.

This is not good advice for an anxiety sufferer. If they are continually worried about how the lack of sleep is affecting their system, what is the point of forcing themselves to keep awake? If they are clocking up the sleepless hours they will be convinced that every minute is building up towards a probable breakdown. Much better to curl up on a sofa and let a pleasant drowsiness take over. It is not necessary to go to bed in a darkened room. Resting in front of an un-demanding television programme is more likely to induce relaxed slumber.

Remember that many of the world's great statesmen, scientists and actors were in the habit of taking time off during the day to recharge their batteries with a refreshing nap.

Sleep phobia

Sleep phobia is always linked with a fear of death, or more likely the fear of the unknown. Where do we go when we are asleep? Is dying a continuation of sleep? 'Losing conscious-ness', 'letting go' as sleep takes over is a frightening thought, even when it happens over and over again. This is a fear that is always present and needs professional help in the way of cognitive therapy to change the sufferer's attitude to the problem and help them to accept sleep as a blessing instead of a threat.

Nightmares

Everyone has nightmares from time to time. These are some-what different to the intense night terrors experienced in connection with panic attacks, but alarming all the same.

As an adolescent I had vivid dreams every night, some bad enough to be called nightmares, some just mildly disturbing.

I tried to avoid dreaming by tying elastic around my waist with a cotton reel held in the centre of my back, under the impression that sleeping on my back made me dream. I endured many uncomfortable nights, reading until the early hours as I found that I was able to sleep only in short bursts. I was relieved when eventually I grew out of dreaming vividly.

Marie (twenty): I had vivid dreams and nightmares for many years. Then one night I dreamed I was in a market square in Elizabethan times, being chased by the queen brandishing an axe and shouting, 'Off with her head!' I persuaded all the villagers to jump up and down as high as they could so that they would bump against my eyelids and wake me up. This worked! I have never been frightened by bad dreams since as I realised I could control them, even though I was asleep.

Make sure that your bedroom is a welcoming place

Part of the following is from my book *Who's Afraid . . . ?*

The self-help experts again advocate keeping your curtains closed at night and clearing your bedroom of unnecessary things such as radio, television and anything that might distract you from sleeping. They tell you that the bedroom is for sleeping only, not reading in bed or any other activity (though they will allow sex).

Now is the time to break a few rules so that you can get away from the feeling that the bedroom is a place where you *must* lie down and go to sleep. If you turn the light out and close the door you will feel that you have shut yourself in a prison from which you won't be able to escape until daylight.

You can do anything you like to change your surroundings, and if you have a sleeping partner you will need to persuade him or her that a bedroom facelift is a good idea. A comfortable armchair, portable television and lots of soothing pictures on the walls will all help to create a relaxed atmosphere.

All too often, children are sent to their bedrooms as a punishment, and this can instil an aversion to bedtime that may persist through life. If you are not comfortable in your bedroom this will obviously affect your sleep. Have lots of comfortable pillows so you can sit up to read, and yes, you can watch television or listen to CDs or the radio, if your partner doesn't object.

Let us touch upon the delicate subject of double beds. Many couples find it impossible to sleep comfortably together but are horrified at the suggestion that they might change to single beds. It is not the beginning of the end as far as marriage or partnership is concerned: there are quite as many couples sleeping in double beds whose marriages are disasters. Pushing two single beds together is a good solution, and if your partner doesn't like the idea, be firm! It is important that your health and well-being come before his or her preferred habits.

Try to go to bed at a regular time, and before you do, make an effort to wind down, directing your attention away from the pressures of the day. A warm bath and a hot drink might help you to relax. Avoid emotional arguments, excitement and intense mental or physical activity (apart from sex) as the more alert and stimulated you are, the longer it will take you to fall asleep.

If you wake in the night try to relax again before you have time to become alert and start to turn over your problems in your mind. Be disciplined and don't allow yourself the indulgence of thinking. Try not to get agitated about whatever woke you because this will cause your body to release the powerful hormones whose task it is to make you alert and ready for action.

If after twenty minutes or so you are still awake and not drowsy, don't fight it. Get up and do something instead of fretting. Make a drink, have something to eat or do something useful. Cool off physically so that when you do go back to your bed it is welcoming and warm. You might feel like going through some relaxation exercises. If you wake around dawn, get up and stay up. Mummy and Daddy aren't going to send you back to bed; you can do what you like.

When you are going through a bad patch, you often find it impossible to drop off to sleep, as each time you are about to waft away you are startled by a flash of acute panic – your heart races and everything seems unreal. You can't control this but it is not a dangerous symptom, so the only way to counteract it is to relax and not let it frighten you. Practise your breathing exercises. If you continually overbreathe it makes sense to realise that you can do this even in your sleep.

What happens then? If you are in a light stage of sleep and your breathing is fast and shallow, all the physical symptoms of anxiety build up (see Chapter 6 on hyperventilation) and you react by having vivid and terrifying dreams. You wake in a state of fear which you attribute to the dreams, but in fact it is the anxiety which comes first. So you can see how important it is to practise until correct breathing is automatic.

Fear of fainting

Almost every phobia sufferer has a dread that their fears will have such a devastating effect on them that they will pass out. But phobics rarely faint. They might feel wobbly and unreal and they might have a morbid fear of losing consciousness, but they don't. Why are they so frightened? Probably one of the reasons is because they feel they would be making an embarrassing spectacle of themselves.

But it wasn't always so. It is worth looking at an earlier attitude towards fainting. In Victorian times, ladies might have practised the art of collapsing gracefully at the feet of an attractive man. Then, fainting or 'swooning' was seen as a sign of gentility and was apparently attractive to the opposite sex. So, at the slightest whiff of scandal, or when they wished to avoid a tedious or embarrassing situation, women simply collapsed.

Jane Austen referred to fainting fits as 'refreshing and agreeable'. If ladies too often fainted they might have been diagnosed as suffering from neurasthenia – a general weakness of the nervous system. (We now know there is no such thing.) The cure was rest, so the ladies spent a lot of their time lying down – which no doubt made them genuinely susceptible to 'funny turns'.

Neuro-developmental delay

In the early days of the last century, Sigmund Freud said he believed that one day someone would find a physical basis for neurosis.

It is accepted that all anxiety states are accompanied by some degree of physical sensation and discomfort caused by an upset of the nervous system. The anxiety triggers off a stress reaction in the body, causing the unpleasant symptoms that the panic attack and agoraphobia sufferers in particular recognise only too well.

Peter Blythe, Director of the Institute for Neuro-Physiological Psychology (INPP) in Chester, has discovered that many agoraphobia sufferers have definite physical characteristics which could, under certain conditions, be a cause of anxiety and panic attacks.

The babies of our primitive ancestors had to cling tightly as their mother swung through the trees or fled from danger – a reflex that was vital for their survival. Today's newborn will still grip firmly to a proffered finger and hang on tightly while being lifted. Babies can swim when only a few weeks old, but by the time they are four months old they have lost the automatic swimming response and will struggle and clutch at adult hands for support.

Thousands of years ago, these and other reflexes were necessary if the baby was to survive, and they still exist today until such time as they are no longer necessary. Some of us, for one reason or another, retain as adults certain infant survival reflexes which should have been controlled by the brain before we were two years old.

If the appropriate adult transformed reflexes have not developed this has an effect on the way the eyes work, on physical co-ordination and balance or a combination of the two. It also results in the person having to continually compensate for the small physical difficulties, which makes them more prone to stress.

When in the past patients have gone to see their doctors and told them, 'I am sure there is something wrong with my eyes because they do not focus properly and I have difficulty in judging distances', or 'At times I see things moving which I know cannot move', this is not further evidence of their being neurotic. The fact is that their eyes are playing tricks on them. In the same way, when other patients have complained about a fear of losing their balance and falling over, when their balance was checked it was found that they had definite co-ordination difficulties.

Sometimes a difficult birth or a feverish illness such as measles or whooping cough can result in a weakened central nervous system caused by brain dysfunction. Many children are affected in this way, and it should not be confused with brain damage but seen rather as a difficulty in controlling functions.

Peter Blythe refers to this condition as neuro-developmental delay (NDD). NDD is not some terrible disability – but the majority of those with NDD find that they are prone to anxiety and other problems.

In her book *Agoraphobia*, Ruth Hurst Vose writes:

> Put very simply: if the reflexes of childhood are not transformed into adult reflexes which are necessary for our proper functions as an adult we are going to be in trouble both emotionally and physically. It has been found that if more than two primitive reflexes are still with us as adults we are much more prone to stress and the disorders this brings.

The INPP will carry out extensive tests for dysfunction in a patient and can also measure the percentage of dysfunction, correcting it with a programme of simple remedial exercises tailored to the individual. The patient is also screened to establish that the problems are due to basic organic faults and are not purely emotional.

Certain apparently unrelated questions do help to pinpoint which part of the nervous system is weakened. See if any of these might apply in your case.

1 Did you have problems in the gym at school?

2 Did you suffer from travel sickness as a child?

3 During school assembly, did you occasionally have the fear that you might faint or fall over?

4 When you are very tired, do you lose co-ordination and become clumsy? Do you drop things, miss the door handle, etc.?

5 Do you become anxious if there are too many people moving about around you, or if too many people talk at the same time?

6 When very tired, do you find that you know what you want to say, but what you actually say is not what you intend?

7 Do you have difficulty in differentiating between left and right?

Peter Blythe is insistent that even when there is a physical basis for agoraphobia and panic disorders, the frightening experiences which the basic physical faults create soon result in the person developing a 'fear of fear' which is indeed neurotic; but that is a secondary neurosis and not a primary one causing the problem.

Patients undergoing NDD therapy are given a series of reflex-inhibition movements which, depending upon what reflexes are found to be incorrect, they do each day for six to fourteen minutes. As they start to get better, the programme may be altered. At the same time many patients on the reflex-inhibition programme do need supportive psychotherapy to deal with the 'fear of fear' which may have developed. Also, they may need some medication during the period in which their system is being corrected. The average time patients are on the programme is a year and its success rate is very promising.

This section owes much to *A Physical Basis for Agoraphobia, The Detection and Treatment* by Peter Blythe and Sally Goddard Blythe. See www.inpp.org.uk for more information.

Depression

Everyone feels sad or miserable sometimes and there will usually be a perfectly good reason for feeling fed up. Bereavement, physical illness, money and relationship worries may all bring on a period of depression. 'I feel so depressed,' we might say, but depressive illness is much more severe than just feeling down.

The word 'depress' means 'to press down', and sufferers often feel that they are living under a black cloud that won't go away. They feel as though they are carrying a heavy weight, their limbs seem heavy and every movement is sluggish and slow. Feelings of helplessness and hopelessness overwhelm them and affect their ability to carry on with normal daily activities.

Those who have never suffered from depression often assume it can easily be shrugged off, and will tell the sufferer to pull himself together or snap out of it, both of which are quite impossible.

Depression is an illness which can affect anyone at any age. It is not connected to and does not develop into insanity. Remember, it is an illness, not a sign of weakness. It doesn't discriminate; it affects men and women regardless of age and background and can often be due to childbirth or the menopause, certain illnesses or viral infections.

It is important for those suffering from depression to seek help as soon as possible. The patient's GP will refer him to a specialist who will be able to determine the appropriate treatment, which may involve psychotherapy, antidepressant medication or both.

For those who are suffering from both depression and anxiety disorder, treatment of the underlying depression may be necessary before treatment of the anxiety can begin.

Amy (twenty): I am a law student and experiencing mild agoraphobia/social phobia. I say 'mild' because I am not housebound but I do have problems coping with acute anxiety in certain situations, mainly when I am travelling and when I am in a group of people in a restaurant or a tutorial. I am worried as it seems to be getting worse. My GP says I am depressed; of course I'm depressed, I am desperately worried about the future and whether I'm ever going to get back to normal again. I had hoped to be referred to a psychiatrist but my doctor has just prescribed antidepressants. I feel I need specialist therapy but all he says is that the waiting lists are very long and he feels the drugs will 'do the trick'.

It is understandable that many patients suffering from anxiety disorder are depressed. PAX members sometimes get quite indignant when their GP suggests they are suffering from depression. Who wouldn't be if they were living with excessive anxiety? Phobias that can disrupt your life and the exhaustion that comes with panic attacks could make even the strongest individual depressed.

These are just a few of the feelings that can threaten to overwhelm the sufferer:

- feeling helpless and hopeless, certain that they will never be happy again;
- unable to sleep at night or the opposite, wanting to sleep all the time;
- feeling agitated and restless;

- being oversensitive and vulnerable, feeling angry without a reason;
- not wanting contact with other people.

If you suffer from depression, remember you are not alone. Contact the self-help organisations who will give you advice and encouragement. Information about these is at the end of this book.

There are a number of things you can do to help yourself:

- Eat properly. You may not feel like eating but you need to keep your strength up and a balanced diet will ensure that you are getting the necessary vitamins to keep you healthy.
- Don't make the mistake of thinking alcohol will help you to relax; it will only worsen the depression and build up more problems for you.
- Exercise may be a word to make you shudder, but surely you can take a turn round the garden or round the block so that you can get a breath of fresh air?
- Make a point of meeting people and chatting to them. If they ask how you are, don't take offence and assume they are being nosey; believe it or not, most people are genuinely concerned if a friend or neighbour is unwell. Tell them if you are going through a bad patch and accept their sympathetic response.
- Let time pass. You can't hasten your recovery, but try to think positively and tell yourself that you will be free of this distressing disorder one day.

13

Triskaidekaphobia
A fear of the number thirteen

So we will go straight on to . . .

14

Doctors, dentists and medical procedures

I find the medicine worse than the malady.
John Fletcher

Doctors

It is unfortunate that many GPs have little sympathy for patients with anxiety disorders. Agoraphobics are told they must make the effort to get to the surgery and wait in the waiting room for their appointment even if they cannot leave their home or sit for half an hour or more in a group of people. Panic attack sufferers, particularly if they are male, are still frequently told, 'Men don't suffer from panic attacks', or even 'There's no such thing as a panic attack.'

'I cannot discuss anything with my doctor,' is a typical protest. 'There is never the time to explain, and if I *have* managed to make the journey to the surgery and had to sit in the waiting room, I am in such a state that I can't remember half the things I wanted to say.'

All too often the problem has to do with lack of communication, when the doctor has little time to deal with a patient who seems incapable of explaining their problem coherently.

Miriam (twenty-seven): My GP is a kind but bluff fatherly type who has little time for 'nervy' women. He talks *at* me but won't give me a chance to explain, so I come away from the surgery feeling I have got nowhere. I try to tell him about my panic attacks and he launches into a three-minute lecture supposed to be reassuring but which just makes me feel guilty about making a fuss.

The way around this difficulty is to put everything down on paper and send your case history to the doctor before making an appointment. Stick to the facts and try not to indulge in self-pity as you list your symptoms, explaining how your life is being affected by anxiety. Wait a day or two before making your appointment, thus giving the doctor time to digest your letter and consider your problem before meeting you face to face. With the information available he should be able to put you at your ease and you will be more relaxed when not having to face a barrage of questions.

You are (outwardly) composed as you sit in the surgery; the doctor has your notes in front of him so that he has a starting-point to work from and is now in a position to make some constructive suggestions about treatment.

First, it is important to establish that there is nothing physically wrong with you, that the wretched symptoms which are so upsetting are the product of your oversensitised nervous system and not a warning of some dreaded disease. The majority of sufferers are convinced that they have weak hearts or some frightening mental illness and it takes sympathetic explanations to reassure them.

In an ideal situation the understanding doctor will explain what is wrong, assuring the patient that they are not going insane, and giving down-to-earth advice and treatment where possible. In so many cases, unfortunately, the doctor himself does not understand the problems associated with panic attacks and phobias and can add to the patient's distress by adopting the all-too-familiar 'snap-out-of-it' attitude or – even worse – 'No one ever died from a panic attack.'

Unfortunately, a panic attack can be so frightening that some people feel they are heading for a terrible climax, and this is when they are inclined to telephone the surgery and demand a visit even though their doctor has told them how to weather such a crisis. It is little wonder in such cases that GPs may appear irritated and unsympathetic.

Often the GP will suggest counselling; perhaps there is a counsellor or practice nurse attached to the surgery. This is a comforting suggestion as the patient feels they need someone who will listen to their problems and not demand any input from themselves. Unfortunately, many counsellors have no professional training in dealing with specific anxiety problems and sufferers become frustrated at the lack of direction.

Hospital waiting lists are long, and patients sometimes have to wait for many months for cognitive behaviour therapy, the most successful way of treating phobias and anxiety disorders (this is explained in Chapter 18). Unfortunately doctors are sometimes not up to date with what is available at local hospitals, and apart from a course of antidepressants they may not suggest any further treatment.

Now, the modern antidepressants work very well on the whole, *but* it is important to have further treatment in order to make a full recovery. This is where the phobia organisations come in. They will be able to tell you what treatment is available in your area and also give you plenty of support and encouragement. They also have their own telephone helplines and, in some cases, therapeutic programmes with the backing of professionals. Details of these organisations are in the final chapter of this book.

If your GP does not know where therapy is available in your area and there are no organisations locally who can help, there is nothing to stop you making your own enquiries. You can telephone or write to the psychiatric department at your nearest hospital and ask if they have a therapy programme for patients with your particular disorder. You can then inform your GP where help is available and ask him for a letter of referral.

At some time your GP will require you to undergo tests to ascertain your general state of health. This will involve taking your blood pressure, a problem with a number of people, not because of the mild discomfort of the procedure but – what is it going to disclose? Is it too high? Too low? What does that mean? Is it serious? All typical reactions from the nervous patient.

Perhaps it will be necessary to check your heart. (Even worse – 'My pulse rate is going through the ceiling!' 'My heart is going to give out at any minute.')

And of course, 'Just pop into the hospital for a blood test.' Not something unduly distressing, you might think, but for some people this is a major obstacle.

Blood

No matter how bad they feel – they might experience dizziness, breathing difficulties, jelly legs – phobia sufferers rarely faint. In a stressful situation their blood pressure rises and effectively prevents them passing out. In contrast, the person with a blood phobia will experience a fall in blood pressure at the sight of blood and they may well faint.

Gina (nineteen): I really hate having injections though I can just about cope if I look the other way so I don't see any blood. Even a tiny drop makes me feel shaky and panicky and I have sometimes fainted when I have cut myself or had a slight accident which resulted in bleeding. It's not just the sight of my blood that starts me off – I have to move away if anyone else is bleeding.

The thought of having to have a blood test is unbearable. At present this isn't a problem but I suppose the time will come when this might be necessary for one reason or another.

I am only nineteen and one thing that really bothers me is the thought of being pregnant and having a baby. I don't think I could possibly face this; it seriously affects my thoughts about my future. I would love to have children and I am not afraid of pain, just the blood. I would have to be anaesthetised before having a blood test and it would be necessary to have a Caesarean section when the time came. Somehow I will have to overcome these problems; please, PAX members, tell me how.

It is thought that fainting at the sight of blood is a throwback reaction to the time when primitive man might 'freeze' in a dangerous situation as an alternative to the 'fight or flight' alternatives. A number of animals react to danger in this way, playing 'dead' in order to discourage further attack by predators who would only attack a moving creature.

Injections

A phobia of injections and certain other medical procedures may also trigger a drop in blood pressure and resulting faint.

Chris (twenty-three): I am a reasonably macho male but since childhood I have had a fear of needles and anything with a sharp point. I can't bear to have a knife pointing in my direction on the dinner table. I must have a very sensitive constitution as I have been in the habit of fainting since I was a teenager.

I cannot describe the traumas I have been through when I have had to have an injection. Sedation is necessary before the hypodermic is produced and I have to look the other way or else I will pass out.

Every day I live in a state of tension in case I have an accident or need to go to hospital for a 'jab' as everyone refers to it in a light-hearted way. I don't find anything light-hearted about it. I know this sounds wimpish but I can't control my reactions and have been told that this is one of the hardest phobias to treat.

Dentists

On a morning TV programme *The Time, The Place*, the audience consisted of dental phobics. Unfortunately these people took over the programme talking about their horrendous experiences, and those waiting on the sidelines to discuss ways of tackling the phobia and learning to over-coming it were left speechless. A very negative experience, but unfortunately many such programmes concentrate more on the sensational aspects of the subject to entertain the viewers.

A dental phobia can be quite devastating. The sufferer may not be able even to face the word 'dentist'. In the past I have been asked to cut out any reference to dentists before sending out the newsletter.

It is a difficult fear to understand, as so many sufferers insist it is not that they are afraid of pain; many of the women had sailed quite happily through childbirth. In fact there is a hoary old legend that a woman will say she would much rather have a baby than undergo dental treatment.

The old view that most dentists don't understand how anxious or phobic people feel is quite incorrect and outdated. Now that dentists are allowed to advertise I suggest that dental phobics take a look through the Yellow Pages. 'Immediate evening appointments for nervous patients whenever possible'; 'Home visits for elderly or anxious patients': 'Special facilities for nervous or anxious patients, including intravenous anaesthetic; sedation; hypnosis' and my favourite: 'Present from the Tooth Fairy'. There are dozens of similar advertisements in my area directory.

Is it the dreaded dentist's chair that bothers you? The old-style chair in which you started by sitting bolt upright while it was cranked backwards was bad enough, but the modern chair is more like an operating table and its very shape can strike fear into the heart. Lying down with your head virtually in the dentist's lap and your feet pointing towards the ceiling can make you feel very vulnerable, dizzy and trapped. An understanding dentist will help you to overcome any aversion to the chair, and many will start treatment with the nervous patient sitting upright on an ordinary chair, gradually transferring to the treatment couch when they have become accustomed to being horizontal and their general fears have subsided.

The examination itself before treatment can be equally

alarming as the dental surgeon taps his way around your teeth, muttering to his assistant. He is only counting teeth and making notes, not about to practise some refined torture you have never dreamed of in your unsuspecting mouth.

Some dentists have abandoned this preliminary mapping of the mouth and leave that until the pressing necessity of treatment has been dealt with, by which time the patient is so relieved that they don't mind the tooth count and check.

Don't forget that the dentist is able to work more quickly and with greater care and accuracy when you are calm and relaxed, and also remember that a relaxed body actually feels pain far less than one that is tensed up.

Hypnotherapy

This is one of the first of the alternative therapies that anxiety sufferers turn to – unfortunately usually in the misguided hope that they can be 'put to sleep' and wake completely free of their symptoms. *Nothing* can do this. The patient has to understand that they must learn what they themselves have to do.

Hypnosis is not sleep. Many people can be hypnotised and remain wide awake and conscious of their surroundings, and it is quite possible for the subject to resist and reject ideas and suggestions made to them by the therapist. Though hypnosis is very helpful in achieving a state of complete relaxation, it is difficult to hypnotise someone who is excessively anxious – the type of person who needs to relax most of all.

Phobic people who hope to find that their fears will just melt away with a snap of the hypnotist's fingers will be disappointed when they find there is still a lot of hard work to be done, learning how to cope with panic and overcome it.

Unfortunately it is the hope of an easy cure which causes

those suffering from anxiety to put themselves at risk in the hands of unqualified practitioners. There are many lay therapists who are excellent, but it is a good rule if you are proposing to consult one of these to do so only on the recommendation of someone who has experience of their techniques.

The British Society of Dental Hypnosis and the British Hypnotherapy Association keep registers of practitioners.

15

Intangible fears

Why I fear I know not; but yet as one deprived
of sense I fear all things.

Ovid

Heights

When does a fear of heights become a problem? What is 'high'? A woman member of *The Open Door* could not sit up to a table, had to sit on a cushion on the floor to eat her meals and found it impossible to walk up more than two stairs without feeling panicky, sick and disorientated.

So many people seem to develop a fear of heights as they grow older. In their youth they would climb mountains, swing from trees, ride on the highest, most terrifying roller coasters; now in middle age they find it difficult to drive across a high bridge or even some coastal roads.

It is not just looking *down*: sometimes looking *up* can be equally disturbing. When my children started to grow adventurous and demanded to go on fairground rides, I would have to stay on the ground and look in the other direction. When my daughter hailed me from the top of a Ferris wheel I was physically sick.

It does seem that inner-ear disorders occur in a huge number of people in later life, causing disorientation and dizziness. A fear of heights can trouble a person as much as any other phobia, though relatively few actually seek treatment; it's just something that they put up with even though it may affect their lives quite seriously.

Training the imagination can help up to a point. If you shut your eyes and walked along an imaginary line on the floor you would have no problem; but visualise a tightrope fifty feet above the ground and it will be virtually impossible to walk along that line. When we are in a situation where we are high up we feel ourselves being drawn towards the edge; we see ourselves plummeting downward, and the inevitable consequences. We have allowed our imagination to get out of control.

Walking on the flat with eyes closed it should be possible to imagine that you are a few inches from the ground and gradually raise the height a little at a time until you can walk steadily an imaginary few feet above the floor.

My brother had a dislike rather than a severe fear of heights and he joined the Parachute Regiment. When training he found that the fear was not there when jumping from an aeroplane, but a balloon tethered to the ground was a different story, and a number of soldiers admitted to unpleasant feelings of queasiness.

Lifts are a problem, but is this a fear of heights or claustrophobia? These fears are also a major part of . . .

Fear of flying

There are reported to be thirty million people in Britain and the USA who suffer from air-travel anxiety. In many cases agoraphobia and claustrophobia are the main problem, not just the mechanics of flying. There is a concern or fear about how they might react – panic or lose control. 'What if I can't bear the feeling of being trapped?' the person might think. 'What if I have a full-scale panic attack? I might scream or faint or make an exhibition of myself.' There is little point in trying to overcome a fear of flying until the basic agoraphobia or claustrophobia has been brought under control.

Air-travel anxiety seminars have lectures on the construction and operation of the aircraft, answering the question at the back of many people's minds: '*How* does it fly?' Acclimatising prospective passengers to the mysteries of flying, particularly those who have never flown before, is the aim of several airlines who run 'no-go' flights. This is exactly like going on a real flight except that the plane doesn't leave the ground.

Dr Maurice Yaffe in the book *Taking the Fear out of Flying* suggests that people practise certain exercises to prepare themselves for the experience. The situations simulate as closely as possible sensations similar to those experienced when actually flying and point out where coping strategies can be applied – for instance, travelling on a crowded underground train or high-speed lift.

As the young Parachute Regiment trainees found, you do not experience the same sensation of height when looking down from an aeroplane as you might from the top of a high building.

Every summer PAX would receive a flurry of letters from

members anxious to go on holiday but afraid to fly. They wanted details of the 'Fly with Confidence' and similar courses so that they might learn to tackle their fears before their holiday. Unfortunately they usually waited until only a couple of weeks before they were due to fly, which hardly gave them enough time to overcome their fears. There is no quick solution, unfortunately.

The founder of the charity Triumph over Phobia (TOP) overcame her fear of flying with the aid of Isaac Marks' book *Living with Fear*. TOP (UK) now runs self-help groups throughout the country under the guidance of Professor Marks.

Wind and weather

Phobias of the elements – sunshine, clouds and large expanses of water – may cause the phobic person to feel disorientated. Many of these phobias would never come to light were it not for the phobia organisations and the media, where people are persuaded to talk about unusual fears.

To admit to having a fear of clouds does not usually engender a very sympathetic response. One sufferer explains her feelings:

> My particular phobia is open sky and clouds. I am happiest on a grey day, even if it is raining, as I can go out quite happily sheltering under an umbrella. I sometimes think I must have been a tortoise or a snail in a past life!
>
> Somehow a canopy of blue sky stretching endlessly over the horizon makes me feel unsafe and dizzy. I don't mind fluffy white clouds if they are not moving much but when they are scuttling across the sky I can't bear to look up.

My real horror is the huge black thunderclouds looming overhead. This may sound trivial but even writing about them makes me feel ill.

For hundreds of years winds have been blamed for upsetting people's equilibrium. Spenser described the north wind as 'bitter, black and blustering', and Shakespeare called it 'wrathful and tyrannous', holding it responsible for 'gout, the falling evil, itch and the ague'. Hundreds of years earlier, Hippocrates was convinced that people exposed to west winds became pale and sickly, with digestive organs that were 'frequently deranged from the phlegm that runs down into them from the head'.

It is likely that there have been wind phobias around for a long time and there is nothing new about them. However, in recent years, in the aftermath of gales that have struck this country, it has been apparent that many many people suffer from these fears. The problem has not been publicised for the simple reason that sufferers endure the fear and keep silent about it.

It has long been known that certain winds peculiar to particular areas of the world can cause strange mental and physical sensations, and with changing atmospheric conditions we in the UK are now feeling the effects of strange winds. These so-called 'witches' winds' around the world have been shown to increase the number of road accidents, violent crimes, suicides and murders, and so have led to an interest in the electricity in the air. When the atmospheric pressure changes, our bodies react to an increased production of adrenalin and metabolism speeds up, blood vessels of the heart and muscles dilate, skin vessels contract, the pupils widen and the hair shows a tendency to stand on end, producing prickles of apprehension. This puts a lot of strain on the system if a wind blows for hours or even days on end; it can be very frightening and we begin to fear that out-of-control feeling – fear of the fear again. However, when we understand that there is a physiological reason for our reactions, much of the anxiety fades.

Thunder and lightning

'It was *such* a thunderstorm,' said the White Queen . . . 'Part of the roof came off, and ever so much thunder got in – and it went rolling round the room in great lumps – and knocking over the tables and things till I was so frightened I couldn't remember my own name.'

Lewis Carroll, *Through the Looking Glass*

Even the most stolid down-to-earth types often overreact during a thunderstorm and hypersensitive people can be overwhelmed by the disturbing stimuli of light and sound. Where there is a concentration of noise and bright light the stimulus can get too much and the nervous system will 'blow a fuse' – in other words, trigger off a panic attack.

The sufferer knows how she is going to feel during the storm, and waiting for it to arrive is almost worse than the actual event.

Here we have to understand the defective perception of time that sufferers of severe anticipatory anxiety experience. During a thunderstorm the period between the lightning flash and the crash of thunder seems endless. The subject asks herself, 'When is it coming? Will I be able to bear it? Will the noise be too great for my ears or for my nervous system to tolerate?' The agonising stress builds up and up and when she finds that she has survived the crash she will start to anticipate the next cycle.

Thunder phobics often believe it is the crack of thunder that they fear most, but during the Second World War when I was a child living in London in the Blitz I was able to see how my mother and grandmother reacted to the deafening noise of anti-aircraft guns and exploding bombs. Both of them were terrified of thunderstorms; they would cover up looking glasses, turn off radios and hide in cupboards, refusing to come out until the storm had passed.

In the dugout air-raid shelter at the bottom of the garden, the women made sure we three children were not distressed by the bombardment. It was noisy but it was exciting, and of course we were safe, they assured us. They showed no sign of fear, and once our ears had adjusted to the racket we even enjoyed a sense of excitement. At the age of ten, I never once felt afraid of air raids.

Those with 'elemental phobias' – thunder, lightning or wind – should recognise that some of the apprehension you feel might well be caused by an oversensitive nervous system reacting to changes in atmospheric pressure.

Coping techniques

Weather forecast sends you into a spin? Don't keep checking them on TV and radio. It is the anticipation, the waiting, that causes the greatest distress.

When do you feel worse? When the lightning flashes? When the thunder rolls? Or during the time when you are awaiting the arrival of the storm? The wait for the first flash of lightning can seem intolerably long and the interval in between the flash and the thunderclap leaves time for anxiety to escalate again and again.

Don't count the seconds between flash and crash!

- Keep your breathing under control. Sit in an easy chair; place your fingertips together on your diaphragm and breathe from the bottom of your lungs; done properly, your fingers should part. Imagine you are blowing up a balloon and watch your tummy inflate.
- Use creative visualisation: try to see your house surrounded by a protective light and tell yourself that you are quite safe, that the sound and light cannot harm you.
- Have ear plugs or cotton wool handy to block the noise. Conversely, many people find it comforting to have soothing music playing in the background. Continue your slow gentle breathing; every time you exhale, let a little more of the tension leave your body. Just imagine your muscles relaxing more and more.

16

Food for thought

Eat, drink and be . . . worried?

Diane (fifteen): My mother is obsessed with healthy eating. She insists that my twin sister and I eat the 'right' sort of food and wants to check absolutely everything that goes into our mouths. She is also worried about us developing anorexia although I have told her that she could be pushing us in that direction with her constant fussing. We aren't allowed to eat anything she regards as junk food and everything must be organic and fresh. She spends hours shopping to ensure that she doesn't make a mistake and feed us anything that might not be absolutely pure. She checks the calories, fat content and additives of everything that goes on the table.

We have all three of us lost weight and my sister and I rely on what we eat at school and buy with our own money to stop us feeling hungry. Of course Mother would like to control this too but we manage to avoid her meddling up to a point. Our father died from cancer two years ago and we wonder if this might have started her obsession.

141

A new eating disorder has raised its ugly head recently. *Orthorexia nervosa* is similar to anorexia nervosa because both involve the restriction of food. While anorexia deals with the limitation of the *amount* and possibly *type* of food, orthorexics focus on the quality of the food, eating only foods that are raw and organic. They are concerned with the type of pesticides or additives that might be present in their food.

Dr Steven Bratman, in his book *Health Food Junkies*, says that people who are obsessed with eating healthily have a real problem and should be taken as seriously as an anorexic or bulimic.

Anorexia nervosa is a disorder most common among adolescent girls in which food avoidance, weight loss, failure of periods and overactivity predominate. Anorexics often display a distorted view of their own bodies, being unable to see how thin they have become. Unsurprisingly, many of them suffer from severe anxiety problems, as the phobia organisations can testify. Treatment is by behaviour modification, supervised weight gain and psychotherapy.

Bulimia nervosa is a variant of anorexia in which meals, often very large meals, are eaten and then vomiting is induced to get rid of them. In a sense the patient with anorexia and bulimia has a severe food phobia, but bulimia is accompanied by bizarre behaviour such as hoarding food, bingeing and self-induced vomiting.

There is no evidence that some foods can have any remedial effect on phobias and anxiety states. Certainly caffeine and nicotine can *cause* anxiety, as can some prescription drugs and certainly some 'recreational drugs' (though it is highly unlikely that any anxiety sufferer would dabble with these). An allergic reaction to certain foods or food additives can also intensify nervous symptoms. The trouble is that many people are looking for a physical reason for their anxiety, always trying to avoid facing the real cause. Nothing a sufferer eats or drinks will 'cure' their nerves.

It is not necessary to study the diets that are forced on us daily by the media. You can't go wrong if you stick to a natural wholefood diet, wholefoods meaning those which have had nothing added and nothing taken away. These are foods which are not processed or refined and are as near to their natural state as possible, and also foods which do not contain artificial additives such as flavourings, colourings or preservatives. Meat should be restricted to one or two meals a week, preferably poultry and lean meat only. Wholemeal bread is important as it contains natural wheat bran.

Unprocessed and unrefined natural foods contain the vitamins and minerals we need, together with fresh fruits and vegetables, beans, pulses and nuts which all contain the fibre necessary for a healthy system.

People with anxiety disorders frequently have a weight problem. Either they are too thin, because their nervous state depresses their appetite so that they eat very little, or at the other end of the scale they have an outsize problem with obesity.

On the whole, too much weight is the greater problem. For every individual who has little appetite because of nervous tension, there are many more who eat for comfort and who – especially if they are stuck in the house all day – will make themselves endless cups of coffee or tea and nibble sandwiches constantly, as well as eating the meals they have prepared for their families.

Agoraphobics who have an aversion to supermarkets or shopping in a central area of the town are more likely to rely on the little shop around the corner, where they feel safe because it is near home and there are unlikely to be crowds of other shoppers. The trouble with corner shops in town or village shops in the country is that they are limited in their stock of foodstuffs, so instead of being able to select the things needed for a well-balanced diet, our agoraphobic mother will have to feed her family on pies, sausages, fish fingers and other convenience foods.

Men have their own problems. Someone who is 'territorially restricted' (mildly agoraphobic) but does not like to admit it, though coping more or less normally and holding down a job may avoid eating in public in pubs or canteens, preferring to eat a solitary sandwich lunch in the office or persuade colleagues to bring in a takeaway meal – with chips.

A problem with weight, whether too much or too little, can be devastating to an agoraphobic woman, who can only too easily develop a poor self-image and let herself go – dreading to see herself in a mirror and feeling progressively more depressed. Oversensitive to the opinions of others, she is even less likely to venture outside the house in case a neighbour comments on the fact that she has lost a lot of weight or else appears to be putting it on. The thin woman will feel tense and miserable and go off her food for the rest of the day; the fat one will comfort herself by drinking more cups of tea and eating more buns and biscuits, her misery increasing along with her girth.

If you are overweight, do avoid crash diets. Their success is only fleeting and you can feel nauseated and physically ill; even worse, all the nervous symptoms can be accentuated in this situation. It is a wise precaution to consult your GP before embarking upon any weight-reducing programme.

Added to the overweight agoraphobic's troubles is the fact that probably she is not getting enough exercise. 'I feel so much worse if I try to exercise,' she will protest. There is a reason for this, of course, because during even slight exertion the heart speeds up, she becomes warm and may begin to sweat and she starts to overbreathe, which causes her to feel progressively worse. Remember that these symptoms can be controlled, and remember too that gentle exercise cannot harm you; it will tone up the body and help to discharge nervous energy.

17

Obsessive compulsive disorder

Say I am free, I am free.
Horace

Many books are written about phobias and anxiety disorders. Some of these are written by medical experts and others by professional writers. The books are all carefully researched in great detail, but few of the authors have personal experience of the problems; they have not suffered from the agonies of fear . . . and it shows. The reader picks this up straight away and may feel that though the book may be an excellent source of information, the person who wrote it does not understand the devastating effects such fears can have on the sufferer.

This is about obsessive compulsive disorder, OCD, and I have to admit that it is something I have not experienced personally. I have, though, been in contact with many OCD sufferers through TOD and PAX, and I feel I have some understanding of the distress they feel. I am sorry if you think I have not written in enough detail but I would refer you to the end of this book, where there are addresses of helpful organisations and also details of books on the subject written by those who have experienced OCD.

Anxious people are particularly addicted to superstitious practices – not perhaps the ones such as not walking under a ladder, throwing salt over their shoulder or staying in bed on Friday the 13th, but the number of personalised protections with which they surround themselves is endless. At one end of the scale are those whose compulsions have escalated into full-blown OCD and who need professional help to overcome their problems; at the other are the rest of us, who have our own sets of harmless rituals that we rely on to keep us safe throughout each day. We can see how this begins in childhood; the baby with his comfort blanket, the little girl who won't be parted from her doll or teddy bear, the way children will touch objects 'for luck' and chant wishes and 'spells'.

As we get older, particularly if we are prone to anxiety, we build up our own collections of superstitions, those magical protective acts of self-defence.

'If only I behave like this, do it that way, repeat this phrase in my mind, everything will be all right . . .' How many times have you used these excuses to try to impose some order on future events? We become locked into these patterns because we are afraid of what might happen if we deviate from them in the slightest way – we are afraid of uncertainty and we feel that we have to be in control.

OCD is an extremely disturbing affliction. About 2 per cent of the population suffer from it and both sexes are affected equally. It imprisons the sufferer in an unreal world of ritual and fear.

Obsessional thoughts may become a serious problem, when the sufferer continually attempts to control his out-of-control imagination which works overtime where obsessional ideas, thoughts and pictures are concerned. Upsetting visions of murder, rape or accidents concerning his nearest and dearest become impossible to shift and cause much distress.

Claire Weekes, in *Self Help for Your Nerves*, is as reassuring as ever:

> The tired mind seems to lose resilience so that frightening thoughts may seem to cling tenaciously. The bewildered sufferer often makes the mistake of trying to push away unwelcome thoughts or replace them with other thoughts. The more he fights in this way, the tenser he becomes and the more thoughts seem to cling ... Small wonder he despairs as he tries to keep unwanted thoughts at bay.

Dr Weekes explains that it is not the compulsion itself that is frightening – for example, repeating a phrase or humming a tune endlessly – but the *feeling* of being obliged to do it. If you can accept the fact that these thoughts and urges will keep coming, and that you don't have to fight them all the time, they will gradually lose the power to worry you and you won't be so exhausted and frightened.

While some nervously ill people find help in religion, to others it brings no comfort. This can cause havoc in a person dedicated to a religious life, especially when he is plagued by what he thinks are sinful thoughts. Thoughts can be grotesque in an abnormally anxious person when accompanied by mental fatigue ... above all he should not give them undue importance by taking them seriously.

It doesn't matter how much the sufferer dwells on his obsessions if he does so willingly. He must learn to see all thoughts for what they are – only thoughts – and shrink from none of them, however severe the compulsion that accompanies them. It is the fear that accompanies the obsession that is so exhausting rather than the effort of trying to fight it.

Compulsive hand-washing is a common symptom of OCD. One member of PAX had always to keep six bars of soap ready for use in case she ran out. Her hands were red and raw from the continual scrubbing but she just could not help herself. Some people may become so obsessed with cleanliness that they cannot face going to public places such as supermarkets where they might come into contact with another's germs.

Some of those afflicted with OCD may feel a compulsive need to check and re-check that lights and appliances are turned off before they leave home. One member of PAX couldn't leave his house without going through a four-hour ritual, checking doors, light switches and taps in strict order. He had a written list of things which he had to do which ran to eight pages.

18

The way forward

*I don't want to read self-help books and listen to relaxation tapes,
I just want someone to make me better.*

PAX member

All the phobia organisations come across this attitude from
time to time, and sometimes it seems impossible to help these
people who may spend hours every day on the telephone to
the helplines and to their personal contacts. All helpful
suggestions are brushed aside as the poor sufferer wails, 'I
can't.' My old grannie used to say, 'Can't means won't . . .'

It is impossible to get better without some suffering. With
nearly every physical illness recovery can be uncomfortable
and often painful, from an irritating itch as a wound heals to
sometimes agonising physiotherapy to ensure full recovery
from broken bones. Mental and emotional disorders take time
to heal and the patient has to play their part in the recovery
programme.

You may choose to go it alone, but in this case be prepared
to push yourself. Be positive and convince yourself that you

are going to lead a life free from fear. One of the reasons you suffer from anxiety is because you have a powerful imagination. You think negatively, picturing yourself as a loser, someone who can't get it together.

> If you *think* you will fail you *will* fail.

Face your fears

Whatever your fears may be, the way to overcome them is basically the same. Remember, you don't fight fear, you accept it is there, but that it will not hurt you; and as you learn how to handle the tools of your recovery – relaxation, correct breathing, change of attitude – you will slowly defeat the fears, no matter how overpowering they seem to be at the moment.

Banish those negative thoughts that are holding you back, and replace them with a positive determination to overcome the obstacles that sometimes appear so daunting that you feel they are insurmountable.

Getting better does not mean that you will never be anxious again, it means you won't be afraid of the feelings if they do occur because you will have learned how to deal with them.

If you are housebound and suffering from disabling anxiety that is preventing you from living a full life, you do need professional help: medication where necessary, explanation and reassurance that will help to prepare you for the next step.

If therapy is not immediately available it is important to learn how to handle your fears and to keep going if at all possible. Often modern drugs can help to preserve a normal lifestyle while waiting for treatment ... and this waiting can sometimes be for several months.

What a relief! You can sit down and forget about treatment, telling yourself that you don't have to do anything. Your GP has prescribed pills that are working well, giving you some respite from constant anxiety. Why should you upset the status quo by forcing yourself and making yourself miserable?

You won't get better this way. Drugs, however helpful, are only meant to be a stop-gap, holding fears at bay until you are able to face them and deal with them.

While waiting for professional help, this is the time to contact the phobia organisations and see what they have to offer in the way of counselling, and to telephone therapeutic groups. Details of the major organisations are in the following chapter.

Panic attacks, agoraphobia and social phobia have much in common. Avoiding situations where the sufferer experiences discomfort or acute fear can escalate until all the different sorts of anxiety merge. Avoiding places where panic attacks are experienced – gatherings where there is contact with other people, travelling, and situations where there is no immediate way of escape – the sufferer becomes overwhelmed and cannot judge where the original problem began.

How do you face the morning? Are you apprehensive, dreading what the day may bring, the problems you will have to face and the constant worry about how you are going to tackle your fears?

Do you *look* worried? Look at yourself in the mirror and check your expression. You will feel a lot better if you change that, so *smile*.

'Many behavioural problems could be averted if people were persuaded of the importance of smiling,' writes Liz Hodgkinson in her book *Smile Therapy*. 'It would be less easy to become caught in a vicious circle of depression and despair if facial expressions were kept positive. People imagine this is difficult to do but in fact it isn't. Once it is understood that facial expressions really do affect emotions, smile therapy can be put into practice.'

In smiling, only one major muscle is used, whereas in the expression of all the negative emotions such as anxiety, fear, disgust and sadness, very many more muscles are involved. For every facial expression except smiling, the face has to be contorted. The more the face is twisted up into unhappy expressions, the sooner those wrinkles will turn into permanent lines.

After we discussed this theory in the PAX newsletter, a number of members wrote in to say they were practising smile therapy.

Jackie: I didn't realise how glum my face looked in repose until I surprised myself in front of a mirror. I am making a conscious effort to confront my reflection and smile at it several times each day. 'Are you feeling happy?' asked my husband (hopefully). 'No, but I'm trying to look happy,' I said. He laughed, I laughed, but it hit home that usually I don't smile much and look as miserable as I feel.

Another member noted:

I have found that it is important to smile with my mouth slightly open, otherwise I am inclined to clench my teeth and this increases tension. I also keep telling myself, look happy and you will be happy.

Crying and laughing both release tension, but laughter is much better for you and is a quicker, more effective way of relaxing than meditation, exercise or drugs. Laughter can make you feel quite weak because it is a muscle relaxant and counteracts the 'fight or flight' feelings. It is also probably the cheapest therapy there is – and you can do it in the privacy of your own home.

Find something pleasant to contemplate in the day ahead. There must be something to look forward to, even if it is just a favourite television programme, the prospect of talking to a friend or a member of the family, or a tasty meal you will be preparing. These sound trivial but will get your mind working.

Keep a notebook or a diary. For some reason this suggestion never goes down very well with PAX members, who protest that they have never kept a diary and don't like the effort of writing. At the end of the day make a note of the things you have enjoyed, and with any luck you may find the list increasing over the following days.

If you have a good day, no panicky feelings, no dark clouds of despair forming over you, count these as pluses to add to that day's list. As the weeks pass you should accumulate dozens of positive thoughts and expectations you can build on.

Enter into the phobic situation

Most people find that their worst moments take place prior to facing the situation they dread. They visualise all their nightmares materialising and worry about the inevitable onset of a panic attack they feel they might not be able to control. When forcing themselves to confront the situation, they find it is not nearly as bad as they had imagined it was going to be.

Anticipation is always worse than realisation.

Before tackling your fears, whether under the direction of a therapist or on your own, you must make a list of the problems you are going to have to face, in ten steps; in other words, you construct a hierarchy. At the bottom of the list are those things you can already do fairly easily. It is important to put down these simple tasks which you can overcome at an early stage as this will give you a sense of achievement, encouraging you to take the next step.

Gradually you work your way to the top of the list until you reach the final goal, which at present you are convinced you will never be able to reach. I am always hesitant about this list as, knowing the phobic personality only too well, I see some of you preoccupied with the final task, constantly returning to it and thinking, 'Never in a hundred years will I be able to do that.'

Others, of course, may well be inspired by visualising their final objective. This is the right attitude to adopt: if you allow negative images to fill your mind you are doomed to failure.

Panic in the home

Those who suffer from monophobia – the fear of being alone – have a special problem: *nowhere is safe*. A panic attack can occur anywhere in the home if a trusted companion is not on hand to comfort and reassure the person whose out-of-control imagination constantly dwells on disasters that might be threatening those members of the family who are not safely at home. This is known as the *calamity syndrome*.

We all experience *separation anxiety* from time to time. How many times when your child has been late home have you got to the stage of visualising yourself attending his funeral? Your husband hasn't telephoned . . . he must have had a heart attack or crashed the car (or be wining and dining another woman). Why hasn't your daughter telephoned? She must have run off with that dreadful young man, or worse still, been abducted.

Such thoughts crowd the sufferer's mind until they become unbearable and panic rises to an intolerable level – how can you get this under control?

You feel terrible; and as you let your control slip you feel that in the next few minutes you will feel even worse and that something frightful will happen. You cannot imagine yourself ever feeling normal again. Because of this you may try and hang on to other people, seeing them as a lifeline to normality. You then get to the stage of believing that you cannot cope without this lifeline.

But you *can* manage without other people and you must learn to let go of them. You may say, 'I can't stay in the house on my own,' but negative remarks like this will only increase the problem. The first thing you must learn to do is to face up to it in a different way. Tell yourself, 'I feel bad when I am left on my own but this does not mean I can't do it if I try.'

You are not really afraid of being alone: you are afraid of being left with yourself and your fears. You must practise staying with yourself for just five minutes – in a room apart from the family, initially – then staying in the house when everyone goes out. Get out that notebook and write down the length of time you lasted and aim to add another five minutes every few days.

Here I must point out that the monophobic is not always a woman, as many people might imagine. Men too can be confined to their home and cannot be left on their own because of their phobia.

Most of the housebound men who have been in contact with PAX are social phobics and the majority are in their early or mid-twenties. Agoraphobia is frequently an additional obstacle and monophobia sometimes develops as a result of shutting themselves away.

The following suggestions are for the monophobic who wants to construct their own hierarchy. Discard those that are not suitable in your case.

- Get my recording *Panic Attacks*. This is not just another correct breathing and relaxation guide but a friend talking you through panic and showing the way to recovery.
- Each day practise the diaphragmatic breathing exercises (see Chapter 6).
- Also practise relaxation techniques, but ensure someone is with you initially as deep relaxation may bring on a panic attack if you are a beginner and become alarmed at the unfamiliar sensations. As you become more experienced you will learn to enjoy these feelings!
- When you are feeling relaxed, shut your eyes and imagine you are alone in the house. You have nothing to worry about; your family and friends are safe and you are taking the first steps to recovering from your phobia. Do this several times each day.
- Stay in a room alone for five minutes while a companion remains in another room.

This is over-simplifying things, I know, but if your phobia is severe and affecting your life it is important to get professional help, and these suggestions are just a few pointers towards what you might do on the first steps to recovery. On their own they are not a solution; you will need structured treatment and a proper recovery plan. Read the next chapter to find out where help is available.

Social phobia

Julie, aged twenty-eight with a young daughter, described herself as 'friendless'. Her daughter Katie had started at primary school and Julie was finding it difficult to make contact with the other mothers; she described them as 'unfriendly and hostile'.

Julie, I knew, was a very nervous young woman. Her expression was permanently worried and she avoided catching your eye when you spoke to her. Her whole attitude said, 'Keep away from me.'

'Do you ever speak to any of them?' I asked her. 'Have you tried saying good morning, or "Isn't the weather awful?"'

Julie could hardly be described as a social phobic. She was just unsure of herself and very shy. But her attitude was basically the same . . . other people were the enemy; they looked down on her, they didn't want to know; they were unsmiling and prepared to reject any friendly overtures.

Julie failed to appreciate that it was her own attitude she was reading in the other mothers' conduct towards her. Her dilemma was that instead of considering the others, she was thinking about herself the whole time. She was afraid of making the first friendly move in case she was rebuffed.

Her first step was to plan to arrive at the school at least ten minutes before she was due to collect Katie at the end of each day. In this way there would only be one or two other mothers waiting and she wouldn't feel overwhelmed by a crowd.

Smile, she was told. Catch the eye of a stranger and see how they light up when you smile at them. From that point it is simple to respond to questions; after all, mothers have plenty to discuss.

Julie found that although this first step was difficult, within a few days she was mixing with the other mothers, learning to respond to their questions and finding out about them and their families. It made such a difference to Katie, who quickly learned to make friends.

Recognising that you have a problem is the first step to overcoming it. Tackling it in the early stages prevents it from getting out of hand and reaching the point where it seems impossible to contemplate ever leading a normal life.

Julie was able to sort out her difficulties, but had she let them build up she might have found herself in a more serious situation, avoiding contact with other people, imagining they were hostile towards her and finding it increasingly difficult to communicate.

Some people cannot bear to be in the company of others; they may not be able to eat or drink with anyone else looking on, and in some circumstances they may retreat from human contact altogether. Again the agoraphobic element comes in; if you are one of these sufferers you might, like the Japanese young men in an earlier chapter, find that you cannot bear even the company of your parents and close family. How on earth do you begin to tackle this?

Again, the first step is to ensure you are prepared for the task ahead of you. You are able to relax, overcome breathing difficulties and approach the ordeal in a positive state of mind. 'I can and I will' should be your motto.

This is the time to list the obstacles you have to overcome, however small and insignificant they may seem, because it is with these small steps that you approach the greater difficulties.

A success in one phobic situation makes coping in other ones easier. If one dangerous situation seems less frightening, so will all the others. The area in which you can live comfortably begins to expand, just as it shrank in the past when the condition was worsening. Although difficult, this process by which you learn to be unafraid is straightforward. The more time you stay in the phobic situation, the less frightening it becomes.

Decide what your ultimate goal will be and put it at the top of the list. *Don't* keep referring to this or you will be put off and will be so disillusioned you will think it is not worth making the effort.

So begin with the simplest task – preferably something you can just about manage to do, say making a telephone call to a member of the family you can pass the time of day with, avoiding getting involved in any intimate conversation.

Just constructing the hierarchy will make you feel you are doing something productive. The next step will be to actually *do* these things! Perhaps the list will look something like this:

- I will make a telephone call each day to someone who is close to me (or who I would like to be close to me).
- I will talk to my parents or some member of my family.
- I will stay in the room where others are eating a meal.
- I will sit and watch television with the family.
- I will sit at the table and eat with the other members of the household.
- I will talk to a visitor to the house.
- I will eat a meal when a visitor is present.
- I will visit someone else's home, either on my own or with a trusted companion.
- I will be able to eat a meal in a friend's home.
- I will go shopping with a trusted companion.

We have seen examples of two extreme opposite cases of social phobia: the shy woman who felt that everyone disliked her and the housebound man who found it difficult to socialise even with members of his family. There are hundreds of other examples I could quote: the student who could not attend lectures; the office worker who lived in dread of having to speak to her employer; the father who could not bring himself to make a speech at his daughter's wedding . . . these particular problems may seem trivial, but they cause a good deal of distress and can escalate into disaster if not checked.

Agoraphobia

Ready to do battle? Forget it. It is no good attacking agoraphobia with a grim determination to overcome it at all costs. It will just fight back and you will be beaten before you start. If you prepare to fight, your body will tense up and the physical symptoms will overcome you as you prepare for action. Gritting your teeth will only give you pain in the neck, so relax, breathe deeply and keep calm. *Now* you are ready to go.

Put on your jacket and go to the front door. Can't go any further? *It doesn't matter.* It is better to start with the intention of entering a phobic situation and turn back at the last moment (even long before the last moment) than not to start at all.

Tell yourself, 'I have opened the door to the way ahead. I am not going out today but I have made myself ready to go.'

Think of yourself standing on a diving board getting ready to take the plunge. You can't stand there indefinitely, though. Make up your mind and *go.*

All the experts advise, 'Enter the phobic situation and stay in it. Let the panic feelings come and stick it out until they peak and subside . . . and they *will* subside. Do this repeatedly and you will be able to tolerate spending a longer and longer time in the situation.'

This is a very hard approach and is difficult to tackle unless you have a professional therapist to advise you or are following a programme devised by one of the phobia organisations. Even then, some people find it virtually impossible to follow.

Many agoraphobics are struggling to lead a normal life, travelling to work every day and coping with their jobs, trying to hide their phobia and determined that no one will realise that they have a problem. They haven't the time to become involved in a therapeutic programme, they just feel they must keep going and overcome their fears the best way they can. For them a less traumatic approach to recovery might be advisable, even if it takes longer.

'Crutches' are frowned upon today but thirty years ago a member of *The Open Door* dreamed up a character who appeared in TOD newsletters – 'Aggie Phobie'. I make no excuse for reintroducing her here, as she was a role model to many women who identified with her and found her a comfort and, dare I say it, an inspiration.

'Aggie' represented a typical agoraphobia sufferer. She was determined to help herself and kept going with the help of a number of 'crutches': a shopping trolley (well, she was a middle-aged lady) and, in her handbag, a bottle of smelling salts and a packet of extra-strong peppermints. She carried an umbrella to act as a mobile roof and always wore sunglasses she could hide behind. A newspaper or magazine would provide a distraction if she felt panicky feelings building up and she led a small dog on a lead – another distraction, a companion she could talk to. In later years she gratefully carried a Walkman and earphones, and of course, joy of joys, a mobile telephone.

How I would have appreciated a mobile phone in my agoraphobic days. I always carried a purseful of small change so that I could phone home when my knees began to wobble and the world appeared threatening. I dedicated my first book,

Who's Afraid of Agoraphobia?, to my mother 'who talked me out of innumerable telephone boxes'. I constantly needed to make contact with home for assurance that I was not going to drop dead, that I must keep going and that I would reach my office in one piece.

It was important to know I could take a taxi quickly if I needed to escape from a situation where panic threatened. I know this goes against all we are now taught about the mistake of avoidance, but when life has to go on we sometimes have to take other steps. The important thing, after all, is to reach your destination, even though you may have to find ways around getting there.

The Aggie Phobie props of smelling salts and extra-strong mints will jolt you out of rising anxiety. For years I carried a packet of nerve tonic tablets. They had a most disgusting taste but I would tell myself that they were doing my nerves good, therefore I would feel better. They helped me to keep going although I felt unsteady and shaky.

It took me five years to work through agoraphobia, which has never troubled me again after nearly forty years. No doubt I would have made a quicker recovery if I had applied today's theories, facing the panic situation, staying in it and overcoming the fear. Certainly, many sufferers are now recovering this way.

But you are waiting to go it alone. Taking that first step through the front door is hard, but if you haven't done this for a while it is progress and an encouragement to widen your boundaries. Assuming that you have no one to advise you, you must decide whether you will try to break the habit of fear by facing the panic situations and staying in them, knowing this is the right way forward, or taking the easier and longer way round by moving forward one step at a time.

Set yourself a goal – the pillar box around the corner

perhaps, or some place you have not walked to unaccompanied for a while. At first you will be tempted to tackle this exercise in a rush, overbreathing wildly as you scuttle round the corner, touch the pillar box and get back home as fast as you can.

No panic? Great! But why do you feel so grotty? The panic did not materialise but the anticipation of how you *might* have felt was almost as bad as the real thing.

Tackle these feelings the way you would tackle a real panic. You are probably hyperventilating, for a start. Forget that paper bag, sit down, relax and concentrate on diaphragmatic breathing, keeping your chest still while expanding your tummy like a balloon then letting it subside again.

When you feel rested, calm and comfortable, visualise yourself walking over the route you have just covered; see yourself tranquil and confident, breathing normally and walking briskly without hurrying. When – in your imagination – you reach the pillar box, stand there for a few minutes; do not rush home straight away but try and remember little things you might have noticed on your real outing.

Are you ready to try again? You don't have to go as far as the pillar box; even if you take only a few steps away from your house this is a start. Take it calmly, breathe slowly and walk about fifty paces before you turn back. Increase this gradually each time you go out. And don't wait until tomorrow – there is nothing to stop you doing it again in an hour's time.

If at all possible, as you progress take a route round the houses. Walking in a circle means that you're always on the way home! Don't be tempted to do this too quickly; if you get over-confident you will be tempted to rush it and you will find yourself back at square one.

'You suggested that I keep a diary,' a PAX member said to me. 'But I don't know what to write in it.' It is surely not that difficult . . . after all, you could just write 'Monday: good day', 'Tuesday: rotten day', but that's not very positive. Neither should you write, 'Today I am going to walk to the corner', because if you don't make it all the way you will feel you have failed. Wait until the end of the day and look forward to writing, 'Today I reached the corner shop before turning back. I felt a bit rocky but I made it.' Write something positive each day so that you can look back and see how you have progressed.

Concentrate on things that are happening around you so that you are not concerned solely with how you are feeling. It is important to do this every day while you are comfortable and not under pressure to go any further until you are quite ready. Remember, the longer you stay in the situations you dread, the less frightening they will become.

You are not alone. All over the world people are learning how to recover from their fears; professional help is now more accessible, doctors are more understanding on the whole and self-help organisations are appearing everywhere.

I wish you a happy and care-free future.

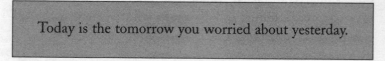

Today is the tomorrow you worried about yesterday.

19

SOS
Where to get help

The phobia organisations

First Steps to Freedom

FSF offers practical help to people suffering from phobias, obsessional compulsive disorders, anxiety, panic attacks, anorexia and bulimia and to those who wish to come off tranquillisers, together with help for their carers.

Helpline

FSF offers a confidential helpline available from 10 a.m. to 10 p.m. 365 days a year for sufferers and carers, to talk over their anxiety problems with trained volunteers who understand how they are feeling and care about them. Each call is treated confidentially; there is practical advice on how to overcome anxiety disorders, or how to overcome withdrawal from tranquillisers.

Telephone self-help groups

FSF provides one-to-one telephone counselling/befriending, whereby a sufferer or carer contacts a volunteer on a regular basis, talks over anxieties, sets themselves goals and steps towards those goals.

FSF also provides leaflets, self-help booklets, videos, audio tapes, etc.

First Steps to Freedom, 1 Taylor Close, Kenilworth, Warks CV8 2LW
Tel: 01926 864473
Website: www.first-steps.org
Helpline: 01926 851608 (10 a.m.–10 p.m., every day)

No Panic

No Panic is a voluntary charity whose aims are to aid the relief and rehabilitation of those people suffering from panic attacks, phobias, OCD and other related anxiety disorders, including tranquilliser withdrawal, and to provide support to sufferers and their families and/or carers by the following means:

- Providing a confidential helpline: Freephone 0808 808 0545, 10 a.m.–10 p.m. every day. Staffed by trained volunteers.
- Providing a night-time anxiety crisis line: Freephone 0808 808 0545, 10 p.m.–10 a.m. every day. Answerphone service only.
- Providing pop-in centres on a regular basis.
- Providing telephone recovery groups.
- Providing a 'contact' booklet service for members wishing to make phone-friends and pen-pals.

- Providing literature, books, audio and video cassettes.
- Providing a written recovery programme for phobias: a simple, easy-to-follow, step-by-step guide to overcoming a phobia.
- Providing support for those trying to give up tranquillisers.
- Providing a telephone-based one-to-one mentoring scheme.
- Providing information designed to raise public and professional awareness of the problems created by anxiety disorders.

No Panic, 93 Brands Farm Way, Telford, Shropshire TF3 2JQ
Tel: 01952 590005
Website: www.no-panic.co.uk
Helpline (Freephone): 0808 808 0545

PAX

Pax is the Latin word for peace. Peace of mind is what everyone is seeking.

PAX is an information and advisory service for those suffering from phobias and anxiety disorders. I started *The Open Door* in 1965 for agoraphobia sufferers with the support of Dr Claire Weekes, author of *Self Help for Your Nerves*, followed by PAX for panic attacks, phobias and other disorders in 1986. Send two loose second-class stamps for information booklet and details of personal telephone counselling service.

The audio tape *Panic Attacks*, which lasts fifty minutes, has helped over two thousand PAX members. In it, I talk the sufferer through panic and guide them through breathing and relaxation techniques, offering comfort and reassurance. It costs £6.00 including postage and packing.

Listening to your voice through the long dark night made me feel I was not alone and that you really did understand what I was going through.

PAX member

PAX, 4 Manorbrook, Blackheath, London SE3 9AW
Website: www.panicattacks.co.uk

National Phobics Society

The National Phobics Society has more than five thousand members who form an extensive self-help network. Across the country, people with anxiety disorders are learning from each other how to cope and how to live with anxiety. The society also publishes factsheets on many different anxiety disorders, some common, some less common. It produces a quarterly newsletter keeping members up-to-date with developments in therapies and self-help strategies, and it offers advice and support by telephone.

Membership costs £15. With this you will also receive four back copies of the newsletter, worth £2.99, plus a free copy of the *NPS Self-Help Guide to Understanding Anxiety*, worth £3.99, and access to the services listed below:

- cognitive behaviour therapy;
- clinical hypnotherapy;
- driving phobia help;
- members' helpline;
- self-help groups;
- quarterly newsletters;
- personal letters and e-mail service;
- contact lists;
- factsheets;
- counselling service.

National Phobics Society, Zion Community Resource Centre, 339 Stretford Road, Hulme, Manchester M15 4ZY
Tel: 0870 7700 456
Website: www.phobics-society.org.uk

Triumph Over Phobia (TOP UK)

TOP UK runs a national network of self-help groups to help people with phobias or OCD to overcome their problems using graded self-exposure. This means learning how to face up to your fears in a very gradual and structured way so that eventually anxiety should decrease.

TOP UK was started in 1987 by Celia Bonham Christie MBE, with the help of Professor Isaac Marks MD FRCPsych of the Institute of Psychiatry, London. Celia overcame her fear of flying by following self-exposure instructions from Professor Marks' book *Living with Fear*.

TOP UK groups are run by trained volunteers, most of whom are ex-phobics or ex-OCD sufferers. A structured self-treatment, self-exposure programme is followed by group members using *Living with Fear* as a self-help manual, meeting weekly in a supportive group.

Group members learn how to measure their anxiety, set weekly achievable goals and keep a weekly diary. They return to their group each week to report on their progress. Our records show that if group members persevere with their programme, they can learn to conquer their fears in an average time of 6–7 months and no longer need the support of the group. Some people, of course, especially those with OCD, find that it takes a little longer.

TOP UK, PO Box 1831, Bath BA2 4YW
Tel: 01225 330353
Website: www.triumphoverphobia.com

Saneline

Saneline gives practical information and support to people with mental health problems, their families and friends, and to professionals and voluntary workers. It puts callers in touch with help and services in their own areas, and gives help from 2 p.m. to 12 midnight every day of the year.

Whether as a sufferer, parent or friend, people faced with a mental health problem can find it difficult to get facts about symptoms and treatments or even to find someone to talk to who is sympathetic. Many feel isolated and unaware of the services available. Saneline has been set up to give this information and support.

Saneline
Tel: 0845 767 8000

OCD Action

Formerly Obsessive Action, this is the national organisation for people with obsessive compulsive disorder (OCD), their carers and interested professionals. Leaflets and factsheets are available. Membership/information pack/list of OCD groups in the UK costs £5.00 (cheques to OCD Action).

OCD Action, Aberdeen Centre, Highbury Grove, London N5 2EA
Tel: 020 7226 4000
Website: www.ocdaction.org.uk

SAD

For a free leaflet about light therapy boxes send an s.a.e.

For a more detailed pack with information about the condition and where to get help, send a cheque or PO for £5.00 made out to SADA to the address below.

SAD Association (Seasonal Affective Disorder)
PO Box 989 Steyning BN44 3HG
Website: www.sada.org.uk (See also www.outsidein.co.uk)

Depression Alliance

To help you understand what depression is, the problems associated with it and how other people have learned to cope, we have a quarterly magazine called *A Single Step*, which contains information, helpful suggestions and letters from members that might help you feel less isolated by your depression. Please send an s.a.e. for information.

Depression Alliance, 35 Westminster Bridge Road, London SE1 7JB
Tel: 020 7633 0557
Website: www.depressionalliance.org

Eating Disorders Association

Eating Disorders Association, 103 Prince of Wales Road, Norwich NRI 1DW
Adult helpline: 0845 634 1414 (8.30 a.m.–8.30 p.m. weekdays)
Youthline: 0845 634 7650 (4.00 p.m.–6.30 p.m. weekdays)
Website: www.edauk.com

GUT Reaction

Emetophobia (fear of vomiting)
Website: www.gut-reaction.freeserve.co.uk

Neuro Development Delay

The Institute for Neuro-Physiological Psychology,
Warwick House, 4 Stanley Place, Chester CHI 2LU
Tel: 01244 311 414
Website: www.inpp.org.uk

British Society of Medical and Dental Hypnosis

28 Dale Park Gardens, Cookridge, Leeds LS16 7PT
Tel/fax: 07000 560309
email: nat.office@bsmdh.org
Website: www.bsmdh.org

British Hypnotherapy Association

67 Upper Berkley Street, London W1H 7QX
Tel: 020 7723 4443

Further reading

Bratman, Steven, and Knight, David, *Health Food Junkies* (Broadway Books, 2001)

Goodwin, Donald, *Phobia, the Facts* (Oxford University Press, 1983)

Hodgkinson, Liz, *Smile Therapy* (Macdonald Optima, 1987)

Levinson, Harold, and Carter, Steven, *Phobia Free: A Medical Breakthrough Linking 90% of All Phobias and Panic Attacks to a Hidden Physical Problem* (Little Brown & Co., 1986)

Marks, Isaac, *Fears and Phobias* (British Medical Association, 1969, 1987)

Marks, Isaac, *Living with Fear* (McGraw-Hill, 1978, 2001)

Neville, Alice, *Who's afraid of agoraphobia? Facing up to fear and anxiety* (Arrow, 1986)

Neville, Alice, *Who's afraid? Coping with fear, anxiety and panic attacks* (Arrow, 1991)

Perls, Frederick, *Gestalt Therapy* (Souvenir Press, 1995)

Vose, Ruth Hurst, *Agoraphobia* (Faber, 1986)

Weekes, Claire, *Self Help For Your Nerves: Learn to Relax and Enjoy Life Again by Overcoming Stress and Fear* (HarperCollins, 1995)

Yaffe, Maurice, *Take the Fear out of Flying* (Constable Robinson, 1998)